THIMBLEBERRIES®
Scrap Quilts

Landauer Publishing, LLC

Scrap Quilts

by **Lynette Jensen**

This book was designed, produced, and published
by Landauer Publishing, LLC
3100 101st Street, Urbandale, IA 50322
800-557-2144; 515-287-2144; www.landauerpub.com

President/Publisher: Jeramy Lanigan Landauer
Vice President of Sales and Administration: Kitty Jacobson
Editor: Jeri Simon
Art Director: Laurel Albright
Creative Director: Lynette Jensen
Photographer: Sue Voegtlin
Technical Writer: Sue Bahr
Technical Illustrator: Lisa Kirchoff

We also wish to thank the support staff of the Thimbleberries® Design Studio:
Julie Jergens and machine quilters: Clarine Howe and Connie Albin.

The following manufacturers are licensed to sell Thimbleberries® products:
Thimbleberries® Quilt Stencils (www.quiltingcreations.com); and Thimbleberries®
Sewing Thread (www.robison-anton.com and www.Sulky.com); and
Thimbleberries® Fabrics (RJR Fabrics available at independent quilt shops).

Printed in Canada 10 9 8 7 6 5 4 3 2 1

Library of Congress Control Number: 2013936903

ISBN 13: 978-1-935726-45-6

Introduction

When I first fell in love with quilts, I was most attracted to scrap quilts. I think it was due to my love of fabrics and the combination of many prints and colors in one quilt. Assembling fabrics for a scrap quilt is still one of my favorite things to do.

Designs using small pieces work best for scrap quilts and the more varied the fabrics the better. The projects in this book use fabrics that give the quilter guidance with colors, prints and the actual yardage needed to complete them. This is very helpful for a beginner quilter who may not have a huge stash of fabric scraps. And, for the more experienced quilter with a generous stash of fabric scraps, every quilt element could be represented by a different print. Sometimes it can be a challenge to make scrap quilts blend. I was once told that the more fabrics you use, the easier it is to make the whole scheme work. I think that may be true. I do know it feels great to use up fabric and create a beautiful quilt at the same time. Enjoy the freedom and spontaneity of making a scrap quilt and remember to enjoy the process.

Lynette Jensen

Contents

Fatty, Fatty, 2 x 4 Throw

Fabrics & Supplies

Finished Size: 60 x 72-inches

- 10 fat quarters (18 x 22-inch piece) **ASSORTED PRINTS** for alternate blocks and 4-patch units

- 10 fat quarters (18 x 22-inch piece) **ASSORTED PRINTS** for borders for 4-patch units

- 2/3 yard **COORDINATING PRINT** for binding

- 3-3/4 yards **BEIGE PRINT** for backing fabric

- quilt batting, at least 66 x 78-inches

*Before beginning this project, read through **Getting Started** on page 65.*

Alternate Blocks and 4-Patch Units

Makes 10 alternate blocks
Makes 20 4-patch units

Cutting

From only 10 of the **FAT QUARTERS**:
  Referring to Cutting Diagram:

- Cut 1, 12-1/2-inch square for alternate block

- Cut 8, 3-1/2-inch squares for 4-patch units

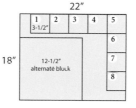

Cutting Diagram for each of the 10 Fat Quarters for the Alternate Blocks and 4-Patch Units

Sew the 3-1/2-inch squares together in pairs; press. Sew the pairs together; press. At this point each 4-patch unit should measure 6-1/2-inches square.

Make 40

Make 20

Borders for 4-Patch Units

Makes 20 pieced blocks

Cutting

From the remaining 10 **FAT QUARTERS**:
- Cut 4, 3-1/2 x 12 1/2-inch rectangles for the side block borders
- Cut 4, 3-1/2 x 6-1/2-inch rectangles for the top/bottom block borders

Note: You can either use the same fabric for all 4 block borders or an assortment of prints for a scrappy look.

Sew the 3-1/2 x 6-1/2-inch rectangles to the top/bottom edges of each of the 4-patch units; press. Sew the 3-1/2 x 12-1/2-inch rectangles to the side edges of each of the Step 1 units; press. At this point each pieced block should measure 12-1/2-inches square.

Make 20

Quilt Center Assembly

Step 1   Referring to the Quilt Center Assembly Diagram, lay out the alternate blocks and the pieced blocks in 6 rows. Sew the blocks together in each row. Press the seam allowances in alternating directions by rows so the seams will fit snugly together. At this point each row should measure 12-1/2 x 60-1/2-inches.

Step 2   Sew the rows together; press. At this point the quilt center should measure 60-1/2 x 72-1/2-inches.

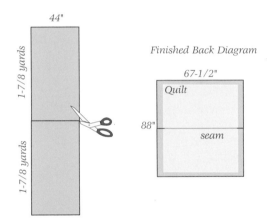

Quilt Center Assembly Diagram

Putting It All Together

Cut the 3-3/4 yard length of backing fabric in half crosswise to make 2, 1-7/8 yard lengths. Refer to *Finishing the Quilt* on page 74 for complete instructions.

44"

1-7/8 yards

1-7/8 yards

Finished Back Diagram

67-1/2"

Quilt

88"

seam

Binding

Cutting

From COORDINATING PRINT:
  • Cut 7, 2-3/4 x 44-inch strips

Sew binding to quilt using a 3/8-inch seam allowance. Refer to *Binding and Diagonal Piecing* on page 75 for complete instructions.

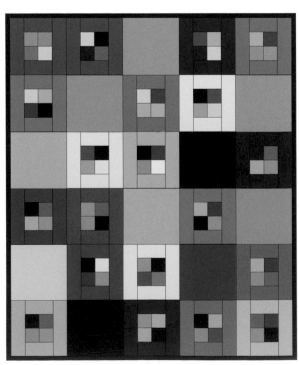

Fatty, Fatty, 2 x 4 Throw
Finished Size: 60 x 72-inches

Color Variation

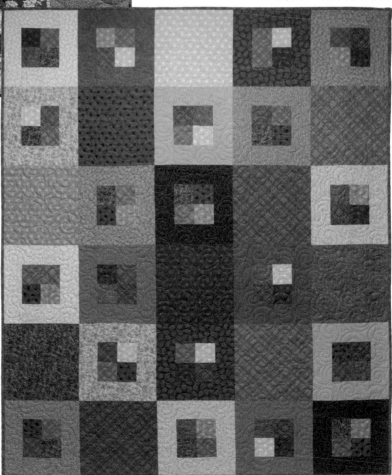

Flying Geese Quilt

Fabrics & Supplies

Finished Size: 100 x 112-inches

- 2/3 yard **ROSE #1** for 4-patch units
- 2/3 yard **GOLD #1** for 4-patch units
- 2/3 yard **ROSE #2** for 4-patch units
- 2/3 yard **GOLD #2** for 4-patch units
- 1/3 yard *each* of **8 MEDIUM PRINTS** for flying geese units (number prints 1 through 8)
- 2-3/4 yards **BEIGE PRINT** for flying geese background
- 1-3/4 yards **BROWN PRINT** for center squares and 3 narrow border strips
- 4-1/4 yards **LARGE FLORAL PRINT** for wide inner/outer borders and narrow middle border
- 1 yard **BROWN** for binding
- 9 yards 44-inch wide backing

OR

- 3-1/4 yards 108-inch wide backing
- quilt batting, at least 106 x 118-inches

Before beginning this project, read through Getting Started on page 65.

4-Patch Units

Makes 42 units

Cutting

From ROSE #1, GOLD #1, ROSE #2 and GOLD #2:
- Cut 5, 4-1/2 x 44-inch strips from *each* fabric

Piecing

Note: Refer to arrows on diagrams for pressing.

Step 1 Sew 4-1/2 x 44-inch **ROSE #1** and **GOLD #1** strips together in pairs. Refer to *Hints and Helps for Pressing Strip Sets* on page 73; press. Make 5 strip sets. Cut strip sets into 4-1/2-inch wide segments.

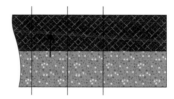

Crosscut 42, 4-1/2-inch wide segments

Step 2 Sew 4-1/2 x 44-inch **ROSE #2** and **GOLD #2** strips together in pairs; press. Make 5 strip sets. Cut strip sets into 4-1/2-inch wide segments.

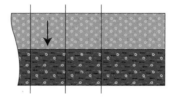

Crosscut 42, 4-1/2-inch wide segments

Step 3 Sew Step 1 and Step 2 segments together in pairs; press. <u>At this point each 4-patch unit should measure 8-1/2-inches square.</u>

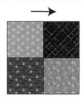

Make 42, 4-patch units

Flying Geese Units

Cutting

From *each* of the #1 through #4 **MEDIUM PRINTS**:
- Cut 4, 2-1/2 x 44-inch strips. From strips cut: 36, 2-1/2 x 4-1/2-inch rectangles

From *each* of the #5 through #8 **MEDIUM PRINTS**:
- Cut 4, 2-1/2 x 44-inch strips. From strips cut: 35, 2-1/2 x 4-1/2-inch rectangles

Flying Geese Quilt

From BEIGE PRINT:
- Cut 36, 2-1/2 x 44-inch strips. From strips cut: 568, 2-1/2-inch squares

Piecing

Note: Refer to arrows on diagrams for pressing.

Step 1 With right sides together, position a 2-1/2-inch **BEIGE** square on the corner of 2-1/2 x 4-1/2-inch **MEDIUM PRINT** rectangle. Draw a diagonal line on the square; stitch on the line. Trim seam allowance to 1/4-inch; press. Repeat this process at the opposite corner of the rectangle.

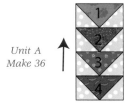

Make 284

Step 2 Referring to the diagrams for color placement, sew together 4 flying geese blocks; press. At this point each flying geese unit should measure 4-1/2 x 8-1/2-inches.

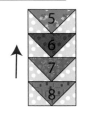

Unit A Make 36 *Unit B Make 35*

Quilt Center Assembly

Cutting

From BROWN PRINT:
- Cut 4, 4-1/2 x 44-inch strips. From strips cut: 30, 4-1/2-inch squares

Piecing

Note: Refer to arrows on diagrams for pressing.

Step 1 For block rows, sew together (6) 4-patch units, (3) A Units and (2) B Units. At this point each block row should measure 8-1/2 x 68-1/2-inches.

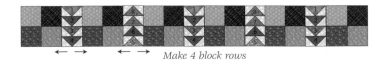

Make 4 block rows

Step 2 For block rows, sew together (6) 4-patch units, (2) A Units and (3) B Units. At this point each block row should measure 8-1/2 x 68-1/2-inches.

Make 3 block rows

Step 3 For lattice strips, sew together (5) 4-1/2-inch **BROWN** squares, (3) A Units and (3) B Units. At this point each lattice strip should measure 4-1/2 x 68-1/2-inches.

Make 6 lattice strips

Step 4 Referring to Quilt Center Assembly Diagram for placement, sew together the block rows and lattice segments; press. At this point the quilt center should measure 68-1/2 x 80-1/2-inches.

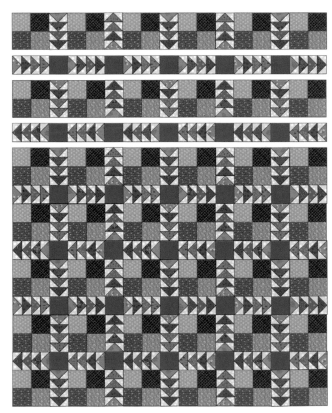

Quilt Center Assembly Diagram

10

Borders

Note: *The yardage given allows for the border strips to be cut on the crosswise grain. Diagonally piece the border strips together as needed, referring to* **Diagonal Piecing** *instructions on page 75. Read through* **Border** *instructions on page 73 for general instructions on adding borders.*

Cutting

From **BROWN PRINT:**
- Cut 27, 1-1/2 x 44-inch narrow inner/middle border strips

From **LARGE FLORAL PRINT:**
- Cut 20, 6-1/2 x 44-inch wide middle/outer border strips
- Cut 9, 1-1/2 x 44-inch narrow middle border strips

Attaching the Borders

Note: *Press seam allowances toward borders just added.*

Step 1   Attach 1-1/2-inch wide **BROWN** inner border strips to the quilt center.

Step 2   Attach 6-1/2-inch wide **LARGE FLORAL** middle border strips to the quilt center.

Step 3   Attach 1-1/2-inch wide **BROWN** middle border strips to the quilt center.

Step 4   Attach 1-1/2-inch wide **LARGE FLORAL** middle border strips to the quilt center.

Step 5   Attach 1-1/2-inch wide **BROWN** middle border strips to the quilt center.

Step 6   Attach 6-1/2-inch wide **LARGE FLORAL** outer border strips to the quilt center.

Border Diagram

Putting It All Together

If you are using 108-inch wide backing fabric, trim the backing and batting so they are 6-inches larger than the quilt top. Refer to *Finishing the Quilt* on page 74 for complete instructions.

If you are using 44-inch wide backing fabric, cut the 9 yard length of backing fabric in thirds crosswise to make 3, 3 yard lengths. Refer to *Finishing the Quilt* on page 74 for complete instructions. The quilt shown was machine quilted with an all over design.

Binding

Cutting

From BROWN:
- Cut 11, 2-3/4 x 44-inch strips

Sew binding to quilt using a 3/8-inch seam allowance. Refer to *Binding and Diagonal Piecing* on page 75 for complete instructions.

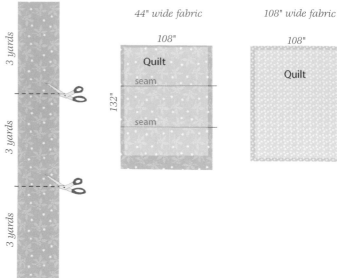

Finished Back Diagram

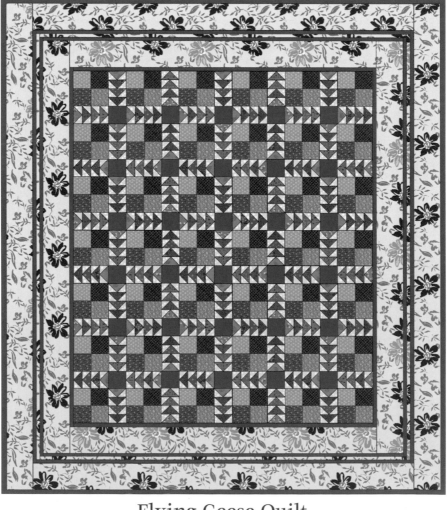

Flying Geese Quilt
Finished Size: 100 x 112-inches

Scrap Patch Paddlewheel Quilt

Fabrics & Supplies

Finished Size: 78 x 90-inches

- 2 yards total **ASSORTED DARK PRINT SCRAPS** for pinwheel blocks

- 2 yards total **ASSORTED BEIGE PRINT SCRAPS** for pinwheel blocks

- 3-3/8 yards total **ASSORTED MEDIUM/DARK PRINT SCRAPS** for sixteen-patch blocks

- 2-5/8 yards **BLACK PRINT** for border and binding

- 7 yards **BEIGE PRINT** for backing

- quilt batting, at least 84 x 96-inches

*Before beginning this project, read through **Getting Started** on page 65.*

Pinwheel Blocks

Makes 71 blocks

Cutting

From **ASSORTED DARK PRINT SCRAPS:**
- Cut 142, 3-7/8-inch squares

From **ASSORTED BEIGE PRINT SCRAPS:**
- Cut 142, 3-7/8-inch squares

Piecing

Step 1   With right sides together, layer the 3-7/8-inch dark print and beige print squares in pairs. Press together, but do not sew. Cut the layered squares in half diagonally to make 284 sets of triangles. Stitch 1/4-inch from the diagonal edge of each pair of triangles; press.

Make 284, 3-1/2-inch triangle-pieced squares

Step 2   Sew the triangle-pieced squares together in pairs; press. Sew the pairs together to make each pinwheel block. <u>At this point each pinwheel block should measure 6-1/2-inches square.</u>

Make 142

Make 71

Sixteen-Patch Blocks

Makes 72 blocks

Cutting

From **ASSORTED MEDIUM/DARK PRINT SCRAPS:**
- Cut 1152, 2-inch squares

Piecing

Step 1   Sew together 4 of the 2-inch squares; press.

Make 288

Step 2   Sew together 4 of the Step 1 units; press. <u>At this point each sixteen-patch block should measure 6-1/2-inches square.</u>

Make 72

Quilt Center Assembly

Step 1   Referring to the Quilt Center Assembly Diagram, sew together the pinwheel blocks and the sixteen-patch blocks in 13 rows with 11 blocks in each row. Press the seam allowances in alternating directions by rows so the seams will fit together snugly with less bulk.

Step 2   Sew the block rows together; press. <u>At this point the quilt center should measure 66-1/2 x 78-1/2-inches.</u>

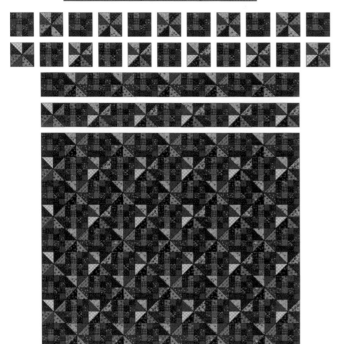

Quilt Center Assembly Diagram

Border

*Note: The yardage given allows for the border strips to be cut on the crosswise grain. Diagonally piece the border strips together as needed, referring to **Diagonal Piecing** instructions on page 75. Read through **Border** instructions on page 73 for general instructions on adding borders.*

Cutting

From **BLACK PRINT**:
- Cut 9, 6-1/2 x 42-inch border strips

Attaching the Border

Attach the 6-1/2-inch wide **BLACK** border strips to the quilt center.

Putting It All Together

Cut the 7 yard length of backing fabric in thirds crosswise to make 3, 2-1/3 yard lengths. Refer to **Finishing the Quilt** on page 74 for complete instructions.

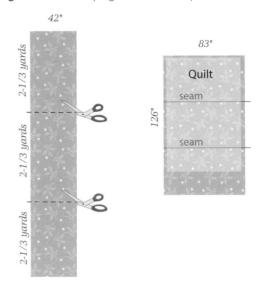

Binding

Note: The 2-3/4-inch wide strips will produce a 1/2-inch wide finished double binding. If you would like a wider or narrower binding, adjust the width of the strips you cut.

Cutting

From **BLACK PRINT**:
- Cut 9, 2-3/4 x 42-inch strips

Sew binding to quilt using a 3/8-inch seam allowance. Refer to **Binding and Diagonal Piecing** on page 75 for complete instructions.

Quilting Suggestion

The border of the quilt was quilted with a crosshatch design. The lines were spaced about 2-inches apart. Since the quilt center is so busy it was quilted with a meander design.

Scrap Patch
Paddlewheel Quilt
Finished Size: 78 x 90-inches

Color Variation

Fruity Tootie Throw

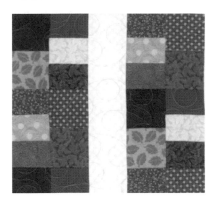

Fabrics & Supplies

Finished Size: 65 x 77-inches

- 3/8 yard *each* MEDIUM BLUE, DARK BLUE, MEDIUM PINK, DARK PINK, YELLOW, GOLD, ORANGE AND DARK GREEN PRINTS for blocks

- 1/2 yard MEDIUM GREEN PRINT for blocks

- 1 yard PURPLE PRINT for blocks and binding

- 3 yards CREAM PRINT for lattice, inner border and outer border

- 4 yards for backing

- quilt batting, at least 71 x 83-inches

Before beginning this project, read through **Getting Started** *on page 65.*

Cutting

From *each* of the DARK BLUE, DARK PINK and YELLOW PRINTS:
- Cut 2, 3-1/2 x 44-inch strips. From strips cut: 23, 2-1/2 x 3-1/2-inch rectangles
- Cut 2, 1-3/4 x 44-inch strips. From strips cut: 5, 1-3/4 x 12-inch border strips

From *each* of the MEDIUM BLUE, MEDIUM PINK and GOLD PRINTS:
- Cut 2, 3-1/2 x 44-inch strips. From strips cut: 22, 2-1/2 x 3-1/2-inch rectangles
- Cut 2, 1-3/4 x 44-inch strips. From strips cut: 5, 1-3/4 x 12-inch border strips

From DARK GREEN PRINT:
- Cut 2, 3-1/2 x 44-inch strips. From strips cut: 22, 3-1/2-inch squares
- Cut 2, 1-3/4 x 44-inch strips. From strips cut: 4, 1-3/4 x 12-inch border strips

From MEDIUM GREEN PRINT:
- Cut 3, 3-1/2 x 44-inch strips. From strips cut: 23, 3-1/2-inch squares
- Cut 2, 1-3/4 x 44-inch strips. From strips cut: 4, 1-3/4 x 12-inch border strips

From ORANGE PRINT:
- Cut 2, 3-1/2 x 44-inch strips. From strips cut: 22, 3-1/2-inch squares
- Cut 2, 1-3/4 x 44-inch strips. From strips cut: 4, 1-3/4 x 12-inch border strips

From PURPLE PRINT:
- Cut 3, 3-1/2 x 44-inch strips. From strips cut: 23, 3-1/2-inch squares
- Cut 2, 1-3/4 x 44-inch strips. From strips cut: 4, 1-3/4 x 12-inch border strips

From CREAM PRINT:
- Cut 7, 6-1/2 x 44-inch strips. Diagonally piece strips to make 4, 6-1/2 x 65-1/2-inch outer border strips
- Cut 8, 3-1/2 x 54-1/2-inch **lengthwise** strips. From strips cut: 6, 3-1/2 x 54-1/2-inch vertical lattice/inner border strips 2, 3-1/2 x 48-1/2-inch top/bottom inner border strips

Block Assembly

Step 1   Lay out (1) 2-1/2 x 3-1/2-inch **DARK BLUE**, **YELLOW** and **DARK PINK** rectangle. Lay out (1) 3-1/2-inch **PURPLE** square and (1) **MEDIUM GREEN** 3-1/2-inch square. Sew the rectangles together; press. Sew the squares together; press. Sew the units together to make Block A. <u>At this point each Block A should measure 6-1/2-inches square.</u>

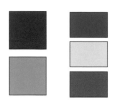

Make 23 Block A

Step 2   Lay out (1) 2-1/2 x 3-1/2-inch **MEDIUM BLUE**, **GOLD** and **MEDIUM PINK** rectangle. Lay out (1) 3-1/2-inch **DARK GREEN** square and (1) 3-1/2-inch **ORANGE** square. Sew the rectangles together; press. Sew the squares together; press. Sew the units together to make Block B. <u>At this point each Block B should measure 6-1/2-inches square.</u>

Make 22 Block B

Pieced Border Assembly

Diagonally piece the 1-3/4 x 12-inch **ASSORTED PRINT** strips together for the pieced borders.

From the DIAGONALLY PIECED STRIP:
- Cut 2, 1-3/4 x 65-1/2-inch side middle border strips
- Cut 2, 1-3/4 x 63-inch side inner border strips
- Cut 2, 1-3/4 x 51-inch top/bottom middle border strips
- Cut 2, 1-3/4 x 48-1/2-inch top/bottom inner border strips

Quilt Center Assembly

Step 1   Referring to Quilt Center Assembly Diagram, lay out (5) Block A and (4) Block B in a vertical row. Sew the blocks together to make Row 1; press. Make a total of (3) Row 1. <u>At this point each block row should measure 6-1/2 x 54-1/2-inches.</u>

Step 2   Referring to Quilt Center Assembly Diagram, lay out (4) Block A and (5) Block B in a vertical row. Sew the blocks together to make Row 2; press. Make a total of (2) Row 2. <u>At this point each block row should measure 6-1/2 x 54-1/2-inches.</u>

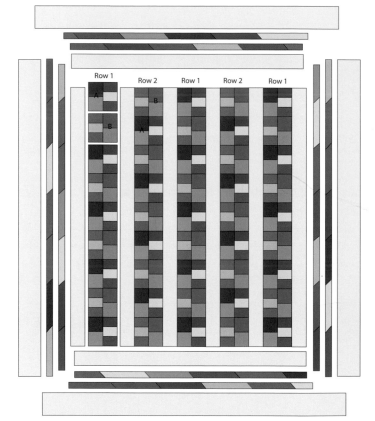

Quilt Assembly Diagram

Step 3   Lay out the (5) block rows and the (6) 3-1/2 x 54-1/2-inch **CREAM** vertical lattice strips. Sew the strips together; press. <u>At this point the quilt center should measure 48-1/2 x 54-1/2-inches.</u>

Borders

Step 1   Attach the 3-1/2 x 48-1/2-inch **CREAM** top/bottom border strips to the quilt center; press.

Step 2 Attach the 1-3/4 x 48-1/2-inch top/bottom inner pieced borders to the quilt center; press. Attach the 1-3/4 x 63-inch side inner pieced borders to the quilt center; press.

Step 3 Attach the 1-3/4 x 51-inch top/bottom middle pieced borders to the quilt center; press. Attach the 1-3/4 x 65-1/2-inch side middle pieced borders to the quilt center; press.

Step 4 Attach the 6-1/2 x 65-1/2-inch **CREAM** outer border strips to opposite sides of the quilt center; press.

Step 5 Attach the 6-1/2 x 65-1/2-inch **CREAM** outer border strips to the top/bottom of the quilt center; press.

Putting It All Together

Step 1 Divide backing into (2) 2 yard lengths. Sew the long edges together; press. The backing seam will be running horizontally to the quilt top.

Step 2 Layer backing, batting and quilt top. Quilt as desired. Our sample was machine quilted with an all over quilt design. Refer to *Finishing the Quilt* on page 74 for complete instructions.

Binding

Cutting

From PURPLE PRINT:
- Cut 8, 2-1/2 x 44-inch binding strips

Sew binding to quilt using a 1/4-inch seam allowance. Refer to *Binding and Diagonal Piecing* on page 75 for complete instructions.

Fruity Tootie Throw
Finished Size: 65 x 77-inches

Three-Patch Runner

Fabrics & Supplies

Finished Size: 16 x 64-inches

- 1/3 yard *each* of **8 ASSORTED PRINTS** for pieced blocks

- 1/2 yard **BLUE DIAGONAL PRINT** for binding

- 1-1/4 yards for backing

Before beginning this project, read through **Getting Started** *on page 65.*

Three-Patch Runner
Finished Size: 16 x 64-inches

Blocks

Makes 4 blocks

Cutting

From *each* of the 8 ASSORTED PRINTS:
- Cut 2, 4-1/2 x 44-inch strips. From strips cut:
  4, 4-1/2 x 8-1/2-inch rectangles
  8, 4-1/2-inch squares

Piecing

Note: Refer to arrows on diagrams for pressing.
Note: Randomly piece the blocks together for a wonderful scrappy runner.

Step 1 With right sides together, position a 4-1/2-inch **ASSORTED PRINT** square on a 4-1/2 x 8-1/2-inch **ASSORTED PRINT** rectangle. Draw a diagonal line on the square; stitch on the line, trim and press. Repeat this process at the opposite corner of the rectangle. At this point each unit should measure 4-1/2 x 8-1/2-inches.

Make 32

Step 2 Sew 8 of the Step 1 units together to make each block; press. At this point each block should measure 16-1/2-inches square.

Step 3 Sew the blocks together end-to-end; press. At this point the runner top should measure 16-1/2 x 64-1/2-inches.

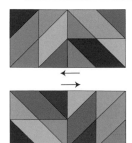

Make 4

Putting It All Together

Step 1 Divide backing into (2) 22-1/2 x 44-inch rectangles. Sew the long edges together; press.

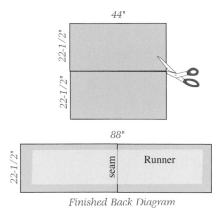

Finished Back Diagram

Step 2 Layer backing, batting and runner top. Quilt as desired. Our sample was machine quilted with an all over quilt design. Refer to *Finishing the Quilt* on page 74 for complete instructions.

Binding

Cutting

From BLUE DIAGONAL PRINT:
- Cut 5, 2-1/2 x 44-inch binding strips

To maintain perfect triangle tips at the outer edges, sew binding to runner using a 1/4-inch seam allowance. This measurement will produce a 3/8-inch wide finished double binding. Refer to *Binding and Diagonal Piecing* on page 75 for complete instructions.

Fireflies Wallhanging

Fabrics & Supplies

Finished Size: 50-inches square

- 1/8 yard *each* of **12 ASSORTED PRINTS** for pieced blocks and pieced border

- 1/3 yard **MEDIUM GOLD PRINT** for "fireflies", flower center/berry appliqués

- 2/3 yard **BEIGE PRINT** for pieced border and small corner squares

- 1/2 yard *each* of **2 LIGHT GOLD PRINTS** for appliqué foundation outer border

- 1/2 yard **MEDIUM GREEN** for large corner squares and leaf appliqués

- 1/8 yard **ROSE PRINT** for flower appliqués

- 1 yard **DARK GREEN PRINT** for vine appliqués and binding

- 3-1/4 yards for backing

- quilt batting, at least 56-inches square

- paper-backed fusible web for flower and leaf appliqués

- tear-away fabric stabilizer

- spray starch (optional)

Before beginning this project, read through **Getting Started** *on page 65.*

Pieced Blocks

Makes 9 blocks

Cutting

Note: Number the **ASSORTED PRINTS** *1 through 12.*

From *each* of the **12 ASSORTED PRINTS:**
- Cut 1, 2-1/2 x 44-inch strip. From each strip, cut:
  1, 2-1/2 x 28-inch strip
  3, 2-1/2 x 4-1/2-inch rectangles (set rectangles aside for pieced border)

From **MEDIUM GOLD PRINT:**
- Cut 1, 2-1/2 x 44-inch strip. From strip cut:
  16, 2-1/2-inch squares

Piecing

Note: Refer to arrows on diagrams for pressing.

Step 1   With right sides together, sew together the #1, #2, #3 and #4, 2-1/2 x 28-inch **ASSORTED PRINT** strips; press. Cut the strip set into 8-1/2" squares.

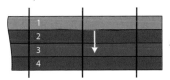

Crosscut 3, 8-1/2-inch squares to make 8-1/2-inch square A pieced blocks

Step 2   With right sides together, sew together the #5, #6, #7 and #8, 2-1/2 x 28-inch **ASSORTED PRINT** strips; press. Cut the strip set into 8-1/2" squares.

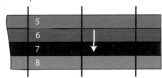

Crosscut 3, 8-1/2-inch squares to make 8-1/2-inch square B pieced blocks

Step 3   With right sides together, sew together the #9, #10, #11 and #12, 2-1/2 x 28-inch **ASSORTED PRINT** strips; press. Cut the strip set into 8-1/2" squares.

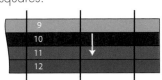

Crosscut 3, 8-1/2-inch squares to make 8-1/2-inch square C pieced blocks

Step 4   With right sides together, position 2-1/2-inch **MEDIUM GOLD** squares on the corners of **2** of the **A** pieced blocks and **2** of the **B** pieced blocks. Draw a diagonal line on each square; stitch on the lines. Trim seam allowances to 1/4-inch; press.

Make 2   *Make 2*
A pieced blocks   *B pieced blocks*

Step 5 Referring to the diagram for block placement, sew the pieced blocks together in 3 rows. Press seam allowances in alternating directions by rows so the seams will fit snugly together with less bulk. <u>At this point each block row should measure 8-1/2 x 24-1/2-inches.</u>

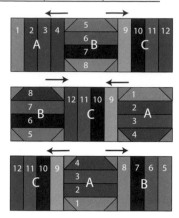

Step 6 Sew the block rows together; press. <u>At this point the quilt center should measure 24-1/2-inches square.</u>

Quilt Center

Cutting

From **BEIGE PRINT**:
- Cut 4, 4-1/2 x 44-inch strips. From strips cut:
  12, 4-1/2 x 8-1/2-inch rectangles
  4, 4-1/2-inch corner squares

From **MEDIUM GOLD PRINT**:
- Cut 1, 2-1/2 x 44-inch strip. From strip cut:
  16, 2-1/2-inch squares

Piecing

Note: Refer to arrows on diagrams for pressing.

Step 1 With right sides together, layer 2-1/2-inch **MEDIUM GOLD** squares on the lower corners of a 4-1/2 x 8-1/2-inch **BEIGE** rectangle. Draw diagonal lines on the squares; stitch on the lines, trim and press.

Make 8

Step 2 Sew Step 1 units to both side edges of a 4-1/2 x 8-1/2-inch **BEIGE** rectangle; press. <u>At this point each unit should measure 4-1/2 x 24-1/2-inches.</u>

Make 4

Step 3 Sew the units to the top/bottom edges of the quilt center; press. Sew 4-1/2-inch **BEIGE** corner squares to both side edges of the remaining units; press. Sew the units to the side edges of the quilt center; press. <u>At this point the quilt center should measure 32-1/2-inches square.</u>

Borders and Appliqué

Note: Yardage given allows for border strips to be cut on crosswise grain. Each outer border strip will be appliquéd individually then the border strips will be sewn together in pairs for each side of the quilt top.

Cutting

*Note: Number the **LIGHT GOLD PRINTS** 1 and 2. The (32) 2-1/2 x 4-1/2-inch **ASSORTED PRINT** rectangles were cut previously.*

From *each* of the 2 **LIGHT GOLD PRINTS**:
- Cut 2, 7-1/2 x 44-inch strips. From strips cut:
  4, 7-1/2 x 18-1/2-inch border strips.

From **BEIGE PRINT**:
- Cut 4, 2-1/2-inch small corner squares

From **MEDIUM GREEN PRINT**:
- Cut 1, 7-1/2 x 44-inch strip. From strip cut:
  4, 7-1/2-inch large corner squares

Piecing

Note: Refer to arrows on diagrams for pressing.

Step 1 For pieced borders, sew together (8) 2-1/2 x 4-1/2-inch **ASSORTED PRINT** rectangles; press. <u>At this point each pieced border should measure 2-1/2 x 32-1/2-inches.</u>

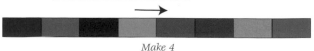
Make 4

Step 2 Sew pieced borders to top/bottom edges of quilt center; press. Sew 2-1/2-inch **BEIGE** corner squares to both edges of remaining pieced borders; press. Sew pieced borders to side edges of quilt center; press. At this point the quilt center should measure 36-1/2-inches square.

Vine Appliqué

Cutting

From DARK GREEN PRINT:
- Cut enough 1-3/4-inch wide *bias* strips to make (8) 20-inch long vines. Diagonally piece strips together as needed.

Appliqué the Vines

Step 1 Fold each 1 3/4 inch wide **GREEN** strip in half lengthwise, wrong sides together; press. To keep raw edges aligned, stitch a scant 1/4-inch away from raw edges. Fold each strip in half again so raw edges are hidden by the first folded edge; press. At this point each vine should measure 1/2 x 20-inches. Set vines aside.

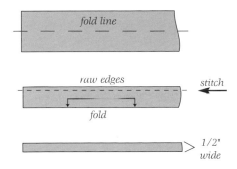

Step 2 Referring to Outer Border Diagram, position prepared vines on the 7-1/2 x 18-1/2-inch **LIGHT GOLD** appliqué foundation border rectangles. When you are pleased with the placement; pin vines in place.

Step 3 We suggest hand basting vines in a zigzag fashion which makes appliquéing so much easier.

Step 4 Using matching thread, edge stitch vines in place.

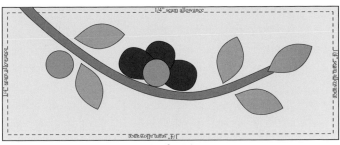

Outer Border Diagram
Make 8

Paper-Backed Fusible Web Appliqué

Step 1 Using the patterns on page 28, trace (24) flower petals, (16) flower centers/berries and (40) leaf shapes on paper side of fusible web leaving a small margin between each shape. Cut shapes apart.

Step 2 Following manufacturer's instructions, fuse the shapes to the wrong side of the fabric chosen for the appliqués. Let the fabric cool and cut along the traced line. Peel away the paper backing from the fusible web.

Note: Spray starch will make your appliqués more stable.

Step 3 Referring to Outer Border Diagram, place the appliqué shapes on outer border rectangles; fuse in place. Machine zigzag stitch around the shapes using matching thread. When the machine appliqué is complete, tear away the stabilizer. If you like, hand blanket stitch the shapes in place with pearl cotton.

Blanket Stitch

Note: To prevent the hand blanket stitches from "rolling off" the edges of the appliqué shapes, take an extra backstitch in the same place as you made the blanket stitch, going around the outer curves, corners and points. For straight edges, taking a backstitch every inch is enough.

Step 4 Referring to the photograph on page 29, sew the appliqued border strips together in pairs; press. <u>At this point each border strip should measure 7-1/2 x 36-1/2-inches.</u>

Step 5 Attach border strips to top/bottom edges of quilt center; press. Sew 7-1/2-inch **MEDIUM GREEN** corner squares to the edges of the remaining border strips; press. Attach border strips to side edges of quilt center; press. <u>At this point the quilt top should measure 50-1/2-inches square.</u>

Putting It All Together

Step 1 Cut the 3-1/4 yard length of backing fabric in half crosswise to make 2, 1-5/8 yard lengths. Refer to the diagram to sew the backing pieces together.

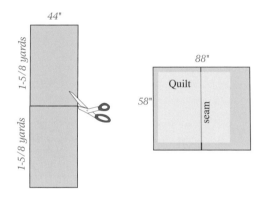

Step 2 Layer backing, batting and quilt top. Quilt as desired. The quilt shown was machine quilted with an all over design. Refer to *Finishing the Quilt* on page 74 for complete instructions.

Quilting Suggestions

- Pieced blocks with **GOLD** triangles - **TB80 - 7-1/2" Star Heart**, in-the-ditch around blocks/**GOLD** triangles

- Pieced blocks (no **GOLD** triangles) - **TB85 - 7-1/2" Heart Swirl**, in-the-ditch around blocks

- **BEIGE** pieced border, corner squares - stipple

- Pieced border - **TB30 - 1-1/2" Beadwork**, in-the-ditch

- **MEDIUM GREEN** corner squares - **TB20 - 7" Tulip**, in-the-ditch

- **LIGHT GOLD** outer border - stipple/meander around applique shapes

- Flower appliqués - in-the-ditch

Binding

Cutting

From DARK GREEN PRINT:
- Cut 5, 2-3/4 x 44-inch strips

Sew binding to quilt using a 3/8-inch seam allowance. Refer to *Binding and Diagonal Piecing* on page 75 for complete instructions.

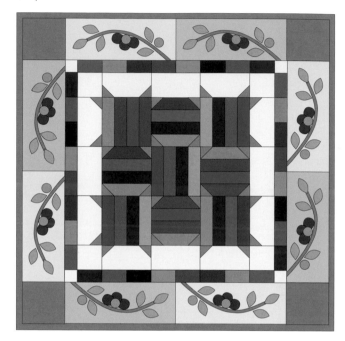

Flower Center/Berry
Trace 16
onto fusible web
GOLD

Flower Petal
Trace 24
onto fusible web
ROSE

Leaf
Trace 40
onto fusible web
MEDIUM GREEN

Fireflies
Finished Size: 50-inches

Color Variation
without Appliqué

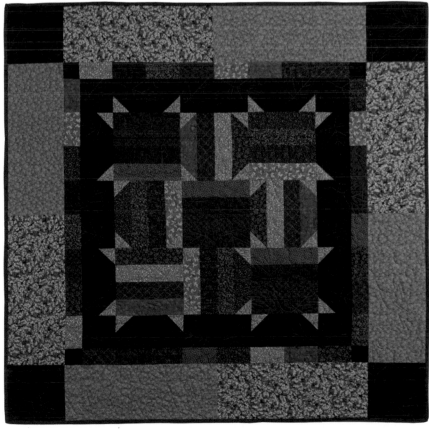

Pinwheel Pillow Sham

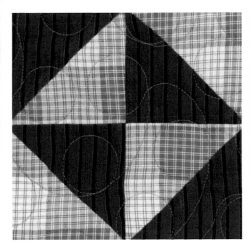

Fabrics & Supplies

Finished Size: 20 x 28-inches

- 5 x 10-inch rectangle of **6 ASSORTED REDS (PRINTS, PLAIDS, STRIPES)** for pinwheel blocks

- 5 x 10-inch rectangle of **6 ASSORTED BEIGES (PRINTS, PLAIDS, STRIPES)** for pinwheel blocks

- 3/8 yard **BROWN PRINT** for border

- 2/3 yard **BEIGE PLAID** for pillow back and pillow back binding

- 1-3/8 yards **BEIGE** for pillow top/back lining

- quilt batting, at least 24 x 31-inches for pillow top

- (2) quilt battings, at least 21 x 24-inches for pillow backs

- 20 x 28-inch pillow form

- spray fabric adhesive (optional)

Before beginning this project, read through **Getting Started** *on page 65.*

Pillow Top

Makes 6 blocks

Cutting

From *each* of the 6 ASSORTED REDS:
- Cut 2, 4-3/8-inch squares from each fabric

From *each* of the 6 ASSORTED BEIGES:
- Cut 2, 4-3/8-inch squares from each fabric

From BROWN PRINT:
- Cut 3, 3-1/2 x 44-inch border strips

From BEIGE:
- Cut 1, 24 x 31-inch rectangle

From quilt batting:
- Cut 1, 24 x 31 inch rectangle

Piecing

Note: Refer to arrows on diagrams for pressing.

Step 1   With right sides together, layer the 4-3/8-inch **RED** and **BEIGE** squares together in pairs. Press together, but do not sew. Cut the layered squares in half diagonally to make 4 sets of each color combination. Stitch 1/4-inch from the diagonal edge of each pair of triangles; press.

Make 4, 4-inch triangle-pieced squares of each color combination

Step 2   Sew 4 triangle-pieced squares together to make each block; press. At this point each block should measure 7-1/2-inches square.

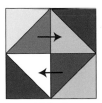

Make 6

Step 3   Sew the blocks together in rows; press. Sew the rows together to make the pillow center; press. At this point the pillow center should measure 14-1/2 x 21-1/2-inches.

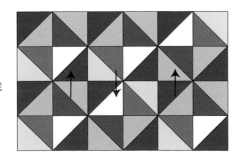

31

Step 4 Referring to *Border* instructions on page 73, attach the 3-1/2-inch wide **BROWN** border strips; press. <u>At this point the pillow top should measure 20-1/2 x 28-1/2-inches.</u>

Quilt the Pillow Top

Step 1 Layer the 24 x 31-inch **BEIGE** lining rectangle, batting and pieced pillow top (right side facing up). To keep the layers stable for quilting, we suggest lightly spraying fabric adhesive on the lining rectangle and batting before layering. <u>Do not spray the pieced pillow top.</u> Pat each layer in place or pin or hand baste the layers together. Quilt as desired. The pillow top shown was quilted with an all over design.

Step 2 <u>Trim quilted pillow top unit to 20-1/2 x 28-1/2-inches.</u> Hand baste edges together to prevent them from rippling when quilted pillow top is sewn to pillow back.

Pillow Back

Note: You will be quilting 2 pillow back rectangles and binding one edge of each.

Cutting

From BEIGE PLAID:
- Cut 1, 18 x 44-inch strip. From strip cut: 2, 18 x 20-1/2-inch rectangles for pillow back
- Cut 1, 2-3/4 x 44-inch strip. From strip cut: 2, 2-3/4 x 22-inch binding strips for pillow back edges

From BEIGE lining and batting:
- Cut 2, 21 x 24-inch rectangles from *each*

Pillow Back Assembly

Step 1 Mark the 18 x 20-1/2-inch **BEIGE PLAID** pillow back rectangles for quilting. The pillow backs in this project were quilted with an all over design.

Step 2 For each pillow back piece, layer a 21 x 24-inch **BEIGE** lining, batting and 18 x 20-1/2-inch **BEIGE PLAID** pillow back rectangle (right side facing up). To keep the layers stable for quilting, we suggest lightly spraying fabric adhesive on the lining and batting before layering. <u>Do not spray the **BEIGE PLAID** pillow back (top layer).</u> Pat each layer in place or pin or hand baste the layers together.

Step 3 Machine or hand quilt the pillow back unit. Trim unit to 18 x 20-1/2-inches. When quilting is complete, hand baste raw edges together a scant 1/4-inch from the edges.

Step 4 Bind *one* edge of the pillow back unit. Fold a 2-3/4 x 22-inch **BEIGE PLAID** binding strip in half lengthwise, wrong sides together; press.

Step 5 With right sides together and aligning raw edges, lay the binding strip on the 20-1/2-inch edge of the pillow back unit. Stitch with a 3/8-inch seam allowance. Turn the folded binding edge over the raw edges and to the back side of the unit. Slip stitch the binding in place.

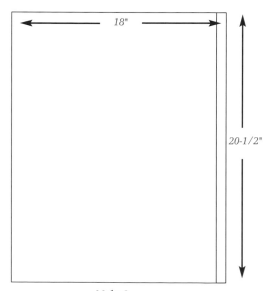

Make 2

Step 6 Repeat to make the remaining pillow back unit.

Step 7 Overlap the 2 prepared pillow back units so the pillow back measures 20-1/2 x 28-1/2-inches. Pin the pieces together and machine baste around entire piece using a 1/4-inch seam allowance to create a single pillow back.

Step 8 With right sides together, layer the pillow back and the pillow top; pin. Stitch around outside edges using a 1/4-inch seam allowance. Turn pillow right side out. Insert pillow form through back opening.

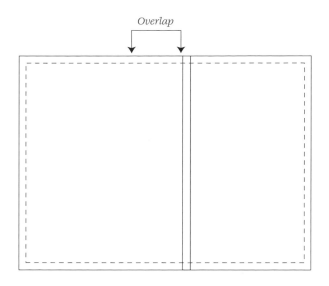

Pinwheel Pillow Sham
Finished Size: 20 x 28-inches

Flying Geese Scrap Quilt

Fabrics & Supplies

Finished Size: 67 x 76-inches

- 1/8 yard *each* of **24 ASSORTED MEDIUM PRINTS** for blocks

- 1/2 yard *each* of **6 ASSORTED BEIGE PRINTS** for block background

- 5/8 yard **ORANGE PRINT** for inner border

- 2-3/8 yards **BLUE PRINT** for lattice and outer border

- 1/8 yard *each* of **7 ASSORTED PRINTS** for pieced binding

- 4-1/4 yards for backing

- quilt batting, at least 73 x 82-inches

Before beginning this project, read through **Getting Started** *on page 65.*

Flying Geese Block

Makes 120 blocks

Cutting

From *each* of the **24 ASSORTED MEDIUM PRINTS**:
- Cut 1, 3-1/2 x 44-inch strip. From strip cut:
  5, 3-1/2 x 6-1/2-inch rectangles
  for a total of 120 rectangles

From *each* of the **6 ASSORTED BEIGE PRINTS**:
- Cut 4, 3-1/2 x 44-inch strips. From strips cut:
  40, 3-1/2 -inch squares for a total of 240 squares

Piecing

Step 1   With right sides together, position a 3-1/2-inch **BEIGE** square on the corner of a 3-1/2 x 6-1/2-inch **MEDIUM** rectangle. Draw a diagonal line on the square; stitch on the line. Trim seam allowance to 1/4-inch; press. Repeat this process at the opposite corner of the rectangle. <u>At this point each flying geese block should measure 3-1/2 x 6-1/2 inches.</u>

Make 120

Step 2   For each block row, sew together (20) flying geese blocks. Press seam allowances up. <u>At this point each block row should measure 6-1/2 x 60-1/2 inches.</u> Make 6 block rows. If the rows are not the same length, adjust the seam allowances as needed.

Lattice, Inner Border and Outer Border

Note: The yardage given allows for the border strips to be cut on the crosswise grain. Diagonally piece the border strips together as needed, referring to **Diagonal Piecing** *instructions on page 75. Read through* **Border** *instructions on page 73 for general instructions on adding borders.*

Cutting

From **ORANGE PRINT**:
- Cut 7, 2-1/2 x 44-inch inner border strips

From **BLUE PRINT**:
- Cut 10, 3-1/2 x 44-inch strips for lattice
- Cut 7, 6-1/2 x 44-inch outer border strips

Quilt Center Assembly

Step 1   Diagonally piece the 10, 3-1/2 x 44-inch **BLUE** strips together in pairs; press. Cut the 5 pieced strips to 60-1/2-inches long (or to the length of your block rows) to make the vertical lattice strips.

Step 2 Referring to the Quilt Assembly Diagram, sew together the block rows and lattice strips to make the quilt center. Press seam allowances toward the lattice strips. <u>At this point the quilt center should measure 51-1/2 x 60-1/2-inches.</u>

Quilt Assembly Diagram

Attaching the Border

Step 1 Attach the 2-1/2-inch-wide **ORANGE** inner border strips to the quilt center.

Step 2 Attach the 6-1/2-inch-wide **BLUE** outer border strips to the quilt center to complete the quilt top.

Putting It All Together

Cut the 4-1/4 yard length of backing fabric in half crosswise to make 2, 2-1/8 yard lengths. Refer to *Finishing the Quilt* on page 74 for complete instructions. We suggest machine quilting the project with an all over design.

Binding

Cutting

From *each* of the **7 ASSORTED PRINTS**:
- Cut 2, 2-3/4 x 44-inch strips. From strips cut: 5, 2-3/4 x 12-inch segments for a total of 35 segments

Piecing

Step 1 With right sides together, diagonally piece the segments together end-to-end in a random fashion to make a long binding strip. Press seams open.

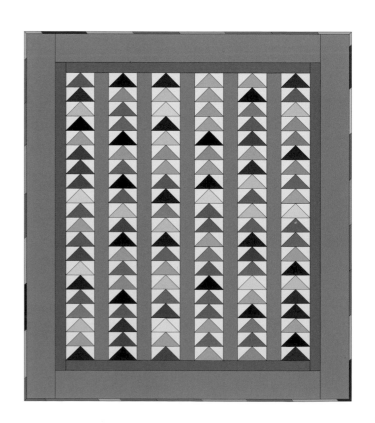

Step 2 Sew binding to quilt using a 3/8-inch seam allowance. Refer to **Binding** and **Diagonal Piecing** on page 75 for complete instructions.

Flying Geese Scrap Quilt

Finished Size: 67 x 76-inches

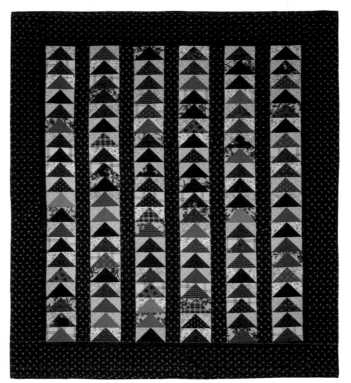

Color Variation

Scrappy Borders and Backings

Joan Arndt of Hutchinson, MN, used the triangle trimmings from her flying geese blocks to create a scrappy border for her quilt.

Dorothy Johnson of Hector, MN, used the leftover scraps from her flying geese quilt to string piece an interesting and unique backing.

Crayon Box Quilt

Fabrics & Supplies

Finished Size: 72 x 90-inches

- 1/4 yard ROSE #1 for triangle-pieced square units
- 1/2 yard ROSE #2 for triangle-pieced square units and pieced border
- 1/4 yard GOLD #1 for triangle-pieced square units
- 1/4 yard GOLD #2 for triangle-pieced square units
- 1 yard LIGHT GREEN for squares
- 2/3 yard each of BEIGE #1, BEIGE #2, BEIGE #3 and BEIGE #4 for block backgrounds
- 1-1/4 yards BEIGE #5 for lattice segments
- 2 yards BEIGE #6 for pieced border
- 1/4 yard BLUE #1 for triangle-pieced square units
- 1/2 yard BLUE #2 for triangle-pieced square units and pieced border
- 1-1/4 yards BROWN for triangle-pieced square units, pieced border and binding
- 1/4 yard CORAL for triangle-pieced square units
- 3/8 yard DARK GREEN for lattice post squares and pieced border
- 5-1/3 yards for backing
- quilt batting, at least 78 x 96-inches

Before beginning this project, read through **Getting Started** *on page 65.*

Block A

Makes 12 blocks

Cutting

From ROSE #1 and GOLD #1:
- Cut 1, 4-7/8 x 44-inch strip from *each* fabric

From LIGHT GREEN:
- Cut 2, 2-1/2 x 44-inch strips

From BEIGE #1:
- Cut 2, 4-7/8 x 44-inch strips
- Cut 3, 2-1/2 x 44-inch strips. From strips cut: 24, 2-1/2 x 4-1/2-inch rectangles
- Cut 2 additional 2-1/2 x 44-inch strips

Piecing

Note: Refer to arrows on diagrams for pressing.

Step 1 With right sides together, layer a 4-7/8 x 44-inch ROSE #1 and BEIGE #1 strip. Press together, but do not sew. Cut layered strip into squares. Cut layered squares in half diagonally to make 12 sets of triangles. Stitch 1/4-inch from the diagonal edge of each pair of triangles; press.

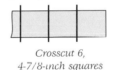

*Crosscut 6,
4-7/8-inch squares*
    *Make 12,
4-1/2-inch triangle-
pieced squares*

Step 2 With right sides together, layer a 4-7/8 x 44-inch GOLD #1 and BEIGE #1 strip. Press together, but do not sew. Cut layered strip into squares. Cut layered squares in half diagonally to make 12 sets of triangles. Stitch 1/4-inch from the diagonal edge of each pair of triangles; press.

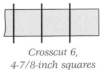

*Crosscut 6,
4-7/8-inch squares*
    *Make 12,
4-1/2-inch triangle-
pieced squares*

Step 3 Aligning long raw edges, sew together the 2-1/2 x 44-inch LIGHT GREEN and BEIGE #1 strips in pairs. Press referring to *Hints and Helps for Pressing Strip Sets* on page 73. Cut strip set into 2-1/2-inch wide segments.

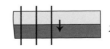

*Crosscut 24,
2-1/2-inch wide segments*

Step 4   Sew a 2-1/2 x 4-1/2-inch **BEIGE #1** rectangle to each Step 3 segment; press. <u>At this point each unit should measure 4-1/2-inches square.</u>

Make 24

Step 5   Referring to the diagram for placement, sew together the Step 1, Step 2 and Step 4 units; press. <u>At this point each block should measure 8-1/2-inches square.</u>

Make 12

Block B

Makes 12 blocks

Cutting

From BLUE #1 and BROWN:
- Cut 1, 4-7/8 x 44-inch strip from *each* fabric

From LIGHT GREEN:
- Cut 2, 2-1/2 x 44-inch strips

From BEIGE #2:
- Cut 2, 4-7/8 x 44-inch strips
- Cut 3, 2-1/2 x 44-inch strips. From strips cut: 24, 2-1/2 x 4-1/2-inch rectangles
- Cut 2 additional 2-1/2 x 44-inch strips

Piecing

Note: Refer to arrows on diagrams for pressing.

Step 1   With right sides together, layer a 4-7/8 x 44-inch **BLUE #1** and **BEIGE #2** strip. Press together, but do not sew. Cut layered strip into squares. Cut layered squares in half diagonally to make 12 sets of triangles. Stitch 1/4-inch from the diagonal edge of each pair of triangles; press.

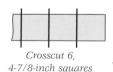

Crosscut 6,   *Make 12,*
4-7/8-inch squares   *4-1/2-inch triangle-pieced squares*

Step 2   With right sides together, layer a 4-7/8 x 44-inch **BROWN** and **BEIGE #2** strip. Press together, but do not sew. Cut layered strip into squares. Cut layered squares in half diagonally to make 12 sets of triangles. Stitch 1/4-inch from the diagonal edge of each pair of triangles; press.

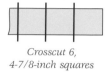

Crosscut 6,   *Make 12,*
4-7/8-inch squares   *4-1/2-inch triangle-pieced squares*

Step 3   Aligning long raw edges, sew together the 2-1/2 x 44-inch **LIGHT GREEN** and **BEIGE #2** strips in pairs. Press referring to *Hints and Helps for Pressing Strip Sets* on page 73. Cut strip set into 2-1/2-inch wide segments. Sew a 2-1/2 x 4-1/2-inch **BEIGE #2** rectangle to each segment; press. <u>At this point each unit should measure 4-1/2-inches square.</u>

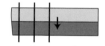

Crosscut 24,   *Make 24*
2-1/2-inch wide segments

Step 4   Referring to the diagram for placement, sew together the Step 1, Step 2 and Step 3 units; press. <u>At this point each block should measure 8-1/2-inches square.</u>

Make 12

Block C

Makes 12 blocks

Cutting

From ROSE #2 and GOLD #2:
- Cut 1, 4-7/8 x 44-inch strip from *each* fabric

From LIGHT GREEN:
- Cut 2, 2-1/2 x 44-inch strips

From BEIGE #3:
- Cut 2, 4-7/8 x 44-inch strips
- Cut 3, 2-1/2 x 44-inch strips. From strips cut: 24, 2-1/2 x 4-1/2-inch rectangles
- Cut 2 additional 2-1/2 x 44-inch strips

Piecing

Note: Refer to arrows on diagrams for pressing.

Step 1 With right sides together, layer a 4-7/8 x 44-inch **ROSE #2** and **BEIGE #3** strip. Press together, but do not sew. Cut layered strip into squares. Cut layered squares in half diagonally to make 12 sets of triangles. Stitch 1/4-inch from the diagonal edge of each pair of triangles; press.

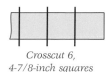

Crosscut 6, 4-7/8-inch squares

Make 12, 4-1/2-inch triangle-pieced squares

Step 2 With right sides together, layer a 4-7/8 x 44-inch **GOLD #2** and **BEIGE #3** strip. Press together, but do not sew. Cut layered strip into squares. Cut layered squares in half diagonally to make 12 sets of triangles. Stitch 1/4-inch from the diagonal edge of each pair of triangles; press.

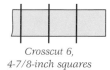

Crosscut 6, 4-7/8-inch squares

Make 12, 4-1/2-inch triangle-pieced squares

Step 3 Aligning long raw edges, sew together the 2-1/2 x 44-inch **LIGHT GREEN** and **BEIGE #3** strips in pairs. Press referring to *Hints and Helps for Pressing Strip Sets* on page 73. Cut strip set into 2-1/2-inch wide segments. Sew a 2-1/2 x 4-1/2-inch **BEIGE #3** rectangle to each segment; press. <u>At this point each unit should measure 4-1/2-inches square.</u>

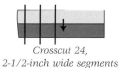

Crosscut 24, 2-1/2-inch wide segments

Make 24

Step 4 Referring to the diagram for placement, sew together the Step 1, Step 2 and Step 3 units; press. <u>At this point each block should measure 8-1/2-inches square.</u>

Make 12

Block D

Makes 12 blocks

Cutting

From CORAL and BLUE #2:
• Cut 1, 4-7/8 x 44-inch strip from *each* fabric

From LIGHT GREEN:
• Cut 2, 2-1/2 x 44-inch strips

From BEIGE #4:
• Cut 2, 4-7/8 x 44-inch strips
• Cut 3, 2-1/2 x 44-inch strips. From strips cut: 24, 2-1/2 x 4-1/2-inch rectangles
• Cut 2 additional 2-1/2 x 44-inch strips

Piecing

Note: Refer to arrows on diagrams for pressing.

Step 1 With right sides together, layer a 4-7/8 x 44-inch **CORAL** and **BEIGE #4** strip. Press together, but do not sew. Cut layered strip into squares. Cut layered squares in half diagonally to make 12 sets of triangles. Stitch 1/4-inch from the diagonal edge of each pair of triangles; press.

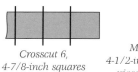

Crosscut 6, 4-7/8-inch squares

Make 12, 4-1/2-inch triangle-pieced squares

Step 2 With right sides together, layer a 4-7/8 x 44-inch **BLUE #2** and **BEIGE #4** strip. Press together, but do not sew. Cut layered strip into squares. Cut layered squares in half diagonally to make 12 sets of triangles. Stitch 1/4-inch from the diagonal edge of each pair of triangles; press.

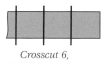

Crosscut 6, 4-7/8-inch squares

Make 12, 4-1/2-inch triangle-pieced squares

Step 3 Aligning long raw edges, sew together the 2-1/2 x 44-inch **LIGHT GREEN** and **BEIGE #4** strips in pairs. Press referring to *Hints and Helps for Pressing Strip Sets* on page 73. Cut strip set into segments. Sew a 2-1/2 x 4-1/2-inch **BEIGE #4** rectangle to each segment; press. At this point each unit should measure 4-1/2-inches square.

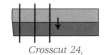

Crosscut 24,
2-1/2-inch wide segments   *Make 24*

Step 4 Referring to the diagram for placement, sew together the Step 1, Step 2 and Step 3 units; press. At this point each block should measure 8-1/2-inches square.

Make 12

Star Block Assembly

Piecing

Note: Refer to arrows on diagrams for pressing.

Step 1 Sew together the A, B, C and D blocks as shown to make each star block; press. At this point each star block should measure 16-1/2-inches square.

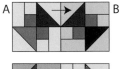 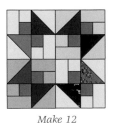

A   B

D   C

Make 12

Lattice

*Note: The yardage given allows for the lattice to be cut on the crosswise grain. Diagonally piece the lattice strips together as needed, referring to **Diagonal Piecing** instructions on page 75.*

Cutting

From BEIGE #5:
- Cut 16, 2-1/2 x 44-inch strips. From strips cut: 31, 2-1/2 x 16-1/2-inch lattice segments

From DARK GREEN:
- Cut 2, 2-1/2 x 44-inch strips. From strips cut: 20, 2-1/2-inch lattice post squares

Quilt Center Assembly

Step 1 For the block rows, sew together (3) star blocks and (4) 2-1/2 x 16-1/2-inch **BEIGE #5** lattice segments; press. At this point each block row should measure 16-1/2 x 56-1/2-inches.

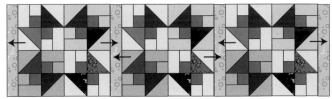

Make 4 block rows

Step 2 For the lattice strips, sew together (4) 2-1/2-inch **DARK GREEN** lattice post squares and (3) 2-1/2 x 16-1/2-inch **BEIGE #5** lattice segments. At this point each lattice strip should measure 2-1/2 x 56-1/2-inches.

Make 5 lattice strips

Step 3 Referring to the Quilt Center Assembly Diagram on page 43, sew together the block rows and the lattice strips; press. At this point the quilt center should measure 56-1/2 x 74-1/2-inches.

Quilt Center Assembly Diagram

Borders

Note: The yardage given allows for the border strips to be cut on the crosswise grain. Diagonally piece the border strips together as needed, referring to **Diagonal Piecing** instructions on page 75. Read through **Border** instructions on page 73 for general instructions on adding borders.

Cutting

From DARK GREEN:
- Cut 2, 2-1/2 x 44-inch strips

From BEIGE #6:
- Cut 4, 6-1/2 x 44-inch strips
- Cut 4, 4-1/2 x 44-inch strips
- Cut 4, 2-1/2 x 44-inch strips
- Cut 4, 2-1/2 x 44-inch strips. From strips cut: 18, 2-1/2 x 8-1/2-inch rectangles

From ROSE #2, BLUE #2 and BROWN:
- Cut 2, 2-1/2 x 44-inch strips from *each* fabric

Pieced Border Assembly

Note: Refer to arrows on diagrams for pressing.

Step 1   Aligning long edges, sew together a 2-1/2 x 44-inch **BEIGE #6** strip, a 2-1/2 x 44-inch **ROSE #2** strip and a 4-1/2 x 44-inch **BEIGE #6** strip. Make 2 strip sets. Press referring to *Hints and Helps for*

Pressing Strip Sets on page 73. Cut strip sets into 2-1/2-inch wide segments.

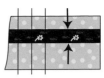

Crosscut 32, 2-1/2-inch wide segments

Step 2   Aligning long edges, sew together a 4-1/2 x 44-inch **BEIGE #6** strip, a 2-1/2 x 44-inch **BLUE #2** strip and a 2-1/2 x 44-inch **BEIGE #6** strip; press. Make 2 strip sets. Cut strip sets into 2-1/2-inch wide segments.

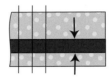

Crosscut 32, 2-1/2-inch wide segments

Step 3   Aligning long edges, sew together a 2-1/2 x 44-inch **BROWN** strip and a 6-1/2 x 44-inch **BEIGE #6** strip; press. Make 2 strip sets. Cut strip sets into 2-1/2-inch wide segments.

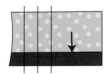

Crosscut 32, 2-1/2-inch wide segments

Step 4   Referring to the diagrams, sew Step 1, Step 2 and Step 3 segments together; press. At this point each unit should measure 6-1/2 x 8-1/2-inches.

Make 14 left side units   *Make 14 right side units*

Step 5   Aligning long edges, sew together a 2-1/2 x 44-inch **DARK GREEN** strip and a 6-1/2 x 44-inch **BEIGE #6** strip; press. Make 2 strip sets. Cut strip sets into segments.

Crosscut 14, 4-1/2-inch wide segments
Crosscut 4, 2-1/2-inch wide segments

Step 6 Referring to the diagram, sew Step 1, Step 2 and Step 3 segments together. Sew 2-1/2-inch wide Step 5 segments to the units; press. <u>At this point each corner unit should measure 8-1/2-inches square.</u>

Make 4 corner units

Step 7 Sew Step 4 right side units and left side units to both side edges of the 4-1/2-inch wide Step 5 segments; press. <u>At this point each unit should measure 8-1/2 x 16-1/2-inches.</u>

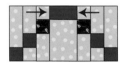

Make 14 units

Step 8 For the top/bottom pieced borders, sew together (3) Step 7 units and (4) 2-1/2 x 8-1/2-inch **BEIGE #6** rectangles; press. <u>At this point each pieced border strip should measure 8-1/2 x 56-1/2-inches.</u> Sew the pieced borders to the top/bottom edges of the quilt center; press.

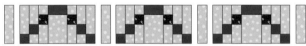

Make 2 for top/bottom pieced borders

Step 9 For the side pieced borders, sew together (4) Step 7 units and (5) 2-1/2 x 8-1/2-inch **BEIGE #6** rectangles; press. Sew Step 6 corner units to the ends of the side pieced border strips; press. <u>At this point each pieced border strip should measure 8-1/2 x 90-1/2-inches.</u> Sew the pieced borders to the side edges of the quilt center; press.

Make 2 for side pieced borders

Putting It All Together

Cut the 5-1/3 yard length of backing fabric in half crosswise to make 2, 2-2/3 yard lengths. Refer to *Finishing the Quilt* on page 74 for complete instructions. The project shown was quilted using an all over design.

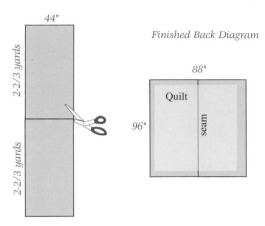

Finished Back Diagram

Binding

Cutting

From BROWN:
- Cut 8, 2-1/2 x 44-inch strips.

To maintain squares at the outer edges, sew binding to quilt using a 1/4-inch seam allowance. This measurement will produce a 3/8-inch wide finished double binding. Refer to *Binding* and *Diagonal Piecing* on page 75 for complete instructions.

Crayon Box Quilt
Finished Size: 72 x 90-inches

Crayon Box Wall Quilt

Fabrics & Supplies

Finished Size: 36 x 45-inches

- 1/8 yard **PLUM #1** for triangle-pieced square units
- 1/8 yard **DARK GOLD** for triangle-pieced square units
- 1/2 yard **GOLD FLORAL** for squares
- 1/4 yard **BEIGE #1** for background
- 1/8 yard **CORAL #1** for triangle-pieced square units
- 1/4 yard **GREEN #1** for triangle-pieced square units and pieced border
- 1/4 yard **BEIGE #2** for background
- 1/4 yard **PLUM #2** for triangle-pieced square units and pieced border
- 1/4 yard **BROWN/GOLD** for triangle-pieced square units and pieced border
- 1/4 yard **BEIGE #3** for background
- 1/8 yard **CORAL #2** for triangle-pieced square units
- 1/8 yard **GREEN #2** for triangle-pieced square units
- 1/4 yard **BEIGE #4** for background
- 1/8 yard **BLACK** for lattice post squares and pieced border
- 3/8 yard **BEIGE #5** for lattice segments
- 1 yard **BEIGE #6** for pieced border
- 1/3 yard **GREEN #3** for binding
- 1-1/2 yards for backing
- quilt batting, at least 42 x 51-inches

Before beginning this project, read through **Getting Started** *on page 65.*

Block A

Makes 12 blocks

Cutting

From PLUM #1 and DARK GOLD:
- Cut 1, 2-7/8 x 20-inch strip from *each* fabric

From GOLD FLORAL:
- Cut 1, 1-1/2 x 44-inch strip

From BEIGE #1:
- Cut 1, 2-7/8 x 44-inch strip. From strip cut: 2, 2-7/8 x 20-inch strips
- Cut 2, 1-1/2 x 44-inch strips. From strips cut: 24, 1-1/2 x 2-1/2-inch rectangles
- Cut 1 additional 1-1/2 x 44-inch strip

Piecing

Note: Refer to arrows on diagrams for pressing.

Step 1 With right sides together, layer a 2-7/8 x 20-inch **PLUM #1** and **BEIGE #1** strip. Press together, but do not sew. Cut layered strip into (6) 2-7/8-inch squares. Cut layered squares in half diagonally to make 12 sets of triangles. Stitch 1/4-inch from diagonal edge of each pair of triangles; press.

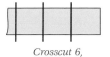

Crosscut 6, 2-7/8-inch squares   *Make 12, 2-1/2-inch triangle-pieced squares*

Step 2 With right sides together, layer a 2-7/8 x 20-inch **DARK GOLD** and **BEIGE #1** strip. Press together, but do not sew. Cut layered strip into (6) 2-7/8-inch squares. Cut layered squares in half diagonally to make 12 sets of triangles. Stitch 1/4-inch from diagonal edge of each pair of triangles; press.

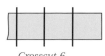

Crosscut 6, 2-7/8-inch squares   *Make 12, 2-1/2-inch triangle-pieced squares*

Step 3 Aligning long raw edges, sew together the 1-1/2 x 44-inch **GOLD FLORAL** and **BEIGE #1** strips in pairs. Press referring to *Hints and Helps for Pressing Strip Sets* on page 73. Cut strip set into 1-1/2-inch wide segments. Sew a 1-1/2 x 2-1/2-inch **BEIGE #1** rectangle to each segment; press. At this point each unit should measure 2-1/2-inches square.

Crosscut 24,
1-1/2-inch wide segments   *Make 24*

Step 4 Referring to the diagram for placement, sew together the Step 1, Step 2 and Step 3 units; press. At this point each block should measure 4-1/2-inches square.

Make 12

Block B

Makes 12 blocks

Cutting

From **CORAL #1** and **GREEN #1**:
- Cut 1, 2-7/8 x 20-inch strip from *each* fabric

From **GOLD FLORAL**:
- Cut 1, 1-1/2 x 44-inch strip

From **BEIGE #2**:
- Cut 1, 2-7/8 x 44-inch strip. From strip cut: 2, 2-7/8 x 20-inch strips
- Cut 2, 1-1/2 x 44-inch strips. From strips cut: 24, 1-1/2 x 2-1/2-inch rectangles
- Cut 1 additional 1-1/2 x 44-inch strip

Piecing

Note: Refer to arrows on diagrams for pressing.

Step 1 With right sides together, Layer a 2-7/8 x 20-inch **CORAL #1** and **BEIGE #2** strip. Press together, but do not sew. Cut layered strip into (6) 2-7/8-inch squares.

Cut layered squares in half diagonally to make 12 sets of triangles. Stitch 1/4-inch from diagonal edge of each pair of triangles; press.

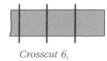

Crosscut 6,
2-7/8-inch squares

Make 12,
2-1/2-inch triangle-pieced squares

Step 2 With right sides together, Layer a 2-7/8 x 20-inch **GREEN #1** and **BEIGE #2** strip. Press together, but do not sew. Cut layered strip into (6) 2-7/8-inch squares. Cut layered squares in half diagonally to make 12 sets of triangles. Stitch 1/4-inch from diagonal edge of each pair of triangles; press.

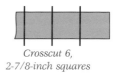

Crosscut 6,
2-7/8-inch squares

Make 12,
2-1/2-inch triangle-pieced squares

Step 3 Aligning long raw edges, sew together the 1-1/2 x 44-inch **GOLD FLORAL** and **BEIGE #2** strips in pairs. Press referring to *Hints and Helps for Pressing Strip Sets* on page 73. Cut strip set into 1-1/2-inch wide segments. Sew a 2-1/2 x 4-1/2-inch **BEIGE #2** rectangle to each segment; press. At this point each unit should measure 2-1/2-inches square.

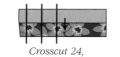

Crosscut 24,
1-1/2-inch wide segments   *Make 24*

Step 4 Referring to the diagram for placement, sew together the Step 1, Step 2 and Step 3 units; press. At this point each block should measure 4-1/2-inches square.

Make 12

Block C

Makes 12 blocks

Cutting

From PLUM #2 and BROWN/GOLD:
- Cut 1, 2-7/8 x 20-inch strip from *each* fabric

From GOLD FLORAL:
- Cut 1, 1-1/2 x 44-inch strip

From BEIGE #3:
- Cut 1, 2-7/8 x 44-inch strip. From strip cut: 2, 2-7/8 x 20-inch strips
- Cut 2, 1-1/2 x 44-inch strips. From strips cut: 24, 1-1/2 x 2-1/2-inch rectangles
- Cut 1 additional 1-1/2 x 44-inch strip

Piecing

Note: Refer to arrows on diagrams for pressing.

Step 1 With right sides together, layer a 2-7/8 x 20-inch **PLUM #2** and **BEIGE #3** strip. Press together, but do not sew. Cut layered strip into (6) 2-7/8-inch squares. Cut layered squares in half diagonally to make 12 sets of triangles. Stitch 1/4-inch from diagonal edge of each pair of triangles; press.

Crosscut 6,
2-7/8-inch squares

Make 12,
2-1/2-inch triangle-
pieced squares

Step 2 With right sides together, layer a 2-7/8 x 20-inch **BROWN/GOLD** and **BEIGE #3** strip. Press together, but do not sew. Cut layered strip into (6) 2-7/8-inch squares. Cut layered squares in half diagonally to make 12 sets of triangles. Stitch 1/4-inch from diagonal edge of each pair of triangles; press.

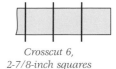

Crosscut 6,
2-7/8-inch squares

Make 12,
2-1/2-inch triangle-
pieced squares

Step 3 Aligning long raw edges, sew together the 1-1/2 x 44-inch **GOLD FLORAL** and **BEIGE #3** strips in pairs. Press referring to *Hints and Helps for Pressing Strip Sets* on page 73. Cut strip set into 1-1/2-inch wide segments. Sew a

1-1/2 x 2-1/2-inch **BEIGE #3** rectangle to each segment; press. At this point each unit should measure 2-1/2-inches square.

Crosscut 24,
1-1/2-inch wide segments

Make 24

Step 4 Referring to the diagram for placement, sew together the Step 1, Step 2 and Step 3 units; press. At this point each block should measure 4-1/2-inches square.

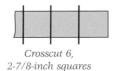

Make 12

Block D

Makes 12 blocks

Cutting

From CORAL #2 and GREEN #2:
- Cut 1, 2-7/8 x 20-inch strip from *each* fabric

From GOLD FLORAL:
- Cut 1, 1-1/2 x 44-inch strip

From BEIGE #4:
- Cut 1, 2-7/8 x 44-inch strip. From strip cut: 2, 2-7/8 x 20-inch strips
- Cut 2, 1-1/2 x 44-inch strips. From strips cut: 24, 1-1/2 x 2-1/2-inch rectangles
- Cut 1 additional 1-1/2 x 44-inch strip

Piecing

Note: Refer to arrows on diagrams for pressing.

Step 1 With right sides together, layer a 2-7/8 x 20-inch **CORAL #2** and **BEIGE #4** strip. Press together, but do not sew. Cut layered strip into (6) 2-7/8-inch squares. Cut layered squares in half diagonally to make 12 sets of triangles. Stitch 1/4-inch from diagonal edge of each pair of triangles; press.

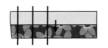

Crosscut 6,
2-7/8-inch squares

Make 12,
2-1/2-inch triangle-
pieced squares

Step 2 Layer a 2-7/8 x 20-inch **GREEN #2** and **BEIGE #4** strip. Press together, but do not sew. Cut layered strip into (6) 2-7/8-inch squares. Cut layered squares in half diagonally to make 12 sets of triangles. Stitch 1/4-inch from diagonal edge of each pair of triangles; press.

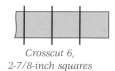

Crosscut 6,
2-7/8-inch squares

Make 12,
2-1/2-inch triangle-
pieced squares

Step 3 Aligning long raw edges, Sew together the 1-1/2 x 44-inch **GOLD FLORAL** and **BEIGE #4** strips in pairs. Press referring to *Hints and Helps for Pressing Strip Sets* on page 73. Cut strip set into 1-1/2-inch wide segments. Sew a 1-1/2 x 2-1/2-inch **BEIGE #4** rectangle to each segment; press. At this point each unit should measure 2-1/2-inches square.

Crosscut 24,
1-1/2-inch wide segments

Make 24

Step 4 Referring to the diagram for placement, sew together the Step 1, Step 2 and Step 3 units; press. At this point each block should measure 4-1/2-inches square.

Make 12

Star Block Assembly

Piecing

Note: Refer to arrows on diagrams for pressing.

Step 1 Sew together the A, B, C and D blocks as shown to make each star block; press. At this point each star block should measure 8-1/2-inches square.

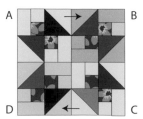

Make 12

Lattice

*Note: The yardage given allows for the lattice to be cut on the crosswise grain. Diagonally piece the lattice strips together as needed, referring to **Diagonal Piecing** instructions on page 75.*

Cutting

From BEIGE #5:
- Cut 8, 1-1/2 x 44-inch strips. From strips cut: 31, 1-1/2 x 8-1/2-inch lattice segments

From BLACK:
- Cut 1, 1-1/2 x 44-inch strip. From strip cut: 20, 1-1/2-inch lattice post squares

Quilt Center Assembly

Step 1 For the block rows, sew together (3) star blocks and (4) 1-1/2 x 8-1/2-inch **BEIGE #5** lattice segments; press. At this point each block row should measure 8-1/2 x 28-1/2-inches.

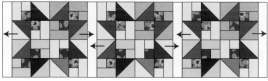

Make 4 block rows

Step 2 For the lattice strips, sew together (4)1-1/2-inch **BLACK** lattice post squares and (3) 1-1/2 x 8-1/2-inch **BEIGE #5** lattice segments. At this point each lattice strip should measure 1-1/2 x 28-1/2-inches.

Make 5 lattice strips

Step 3 Sew together the block rows and the lattice strips; press. At this point the quilt center should measure 28-1/2 x 37-1/2-inches.

Borders

*Note: The yardage given allows for the border strips to be cut on the crosswise grain. Diagonally piece the border strips together as needed, referring to **Diagonal Piecing** instructions on page 75. Read through **Border** instructions on page 73 for general instructions on adding borders.*

Cutting

From **BLACK**:
- Cut 1, 1-1/2 x 44-inch strip

From **BEIGE #6**:
- Cut 3, 3-1/2 x 44-inch strips
- Cut 4, 2-1/2 x 44-inch strips
- Cut 4, 1-1/2 x 44-inch strips
- Cut 2, 1-1/2 x 44-inch strips. From strips cut: 18, 1-1/2 x 4-1/2-inch rectangles

From **PLUM #2, BROWN/GOLD** and **GREEN #1**:
- Cut 2, 1-1/2 x 44-inch strips from *each* fabric

Pieced Border Assembly

Note: Refer to arrows on diagrams for pressing.

Step 1 Aligning long edges, sew together a 1-1/2 x 44-inch **BEIGE #6** strip, a 1-1/2 x 44-inch **PLUM #2** strip and a 2-1/2 x 44-inch **BEIGE #6** strip. Make 2 strip sets. Press referring to **Hints and Helps for Pressing Strip Sets** on page 73. Cut strip sets into 1-1/2-inch wide segments.

Crosscut 32, 1-1/2-inch wide segments

Step 2 Aligning long edges, sew together a 2-1/2 x 44-inch **BEIGE #6** strip, a 1-1/2 x 44-inch **BROWN/GOLD** strip and a 1-1/2 x 44-inch **BEIGE #6** strip; press. Make 2 strip sets. Cut strip sets into 1-1/2-inch wide segments.

Crosscut 32, 1-1/2-inch wide segments

Step 3 Sew together a 1-1/2 x 44-inch **GREEN #1** strip and a 3-1/2 x 44-inch **BEIGE #6** strip; press. Make 2 strip sets. Cut strip sets into 1-1/2-inch wide segments.

Crosscut 32, 1-1/2-inch wide segments

Step 4 Referring to the diagrams, sew Step 1, Step 2 and Step 3 segments together; press. At this point each unit should measure 3-1/2 x 4-1/2-inches.

Make 14 left side units   *Make 14 right side units*

Step 5 Aligning long edges, sew together a 1-1/2 x 44-inch **BLACK** strip and a 3-1/2 x 44-inch **BEIGE #6** strip; press. Cut strip sets into segments.

Crosscut 14, 2-1/2-inch wide segments
Crosscut 4, 1-1/2-inch wide segments

Step 6 Referring to the diagram, sew Step 1, Step 2 and Step 3 segments together. Sew 1-1/2-inch wide Step 5 segments to the units; press. At this point each corner unit should measure 4-1/2-inches square.

Make 4 corner units

Step 7 Sew Step 4 right side units and left side units to both side edges of the 2-1/2-inch wide Step 5 segments; press. <u>At this point each unit should measure 4-1/2 x 8-1/2-inches.</u>

Make 14 units

Step 8 For the top/bottom pieced borders, sew together (3) Step 7 units and (4) 1-1/2 x 8-1/2-inch **BEIGE #6** rectangles; press. <u>At this point each pieced border strip should measure 4-1/2 x 28-1/2-inches.</u> Sew the pieced borders to the top/bottom edges of the quilt center; press.

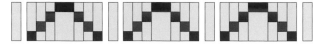

Make 2 for top/bottom pieced borders

Step 9 For the side pieced borders, sew together (4) Step 7 units and (5) 1-1/2 x 8-1/2-inch **BEIGE #6** rectangles; press. Sew Step 6 corner units to the ends of the side pieced border strips; press. <u>At this point each pieced border strip should measure 4-1/2 x 45-1/2-inches.</u> Sew the pieced borders to the side edges of the quilt center; press.

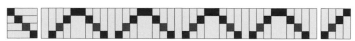

Make 2 for side pieced borders

Putting It All Together

Trim batting/backing so they are 6" larger than the quilt top. Refer to *Finishing the Quilt* on page 74 for complete instructions. The project shown was quilted using an all over design.

Binding

Cutting

From **GREEN #3**:
- Cut 4, 2-1/2 x 44-inch strips.

To maintain squares at the outer edges, sew binding to quilt using a 1/4-inch seam allowance. Refer to *Binding and Diagonal Piecing* on page 75 for complete instructions.

Crayon Box Wall Quilt
Finished Size: 36 x 45-inches

Bubble Woolie Pillow

Fabrics & Supplies

Finished Size: 18-inches square

Note: Extra yardage is allowed so the wool can be felted (prewashed). 100% wool can shrink up to 20% in width and length; a wool blend will shrink less. To avoid future shrinkage upon completion of your wool appliqué project, dry cleaning is recommended.

- 10-inch square **BLACK WOOL** for circles
- 14-inch square **GOLD WOOL** for circles
- 10-inch square **GREEN WOOL** for circles
- 1-1/4 yards **STRIPE PRINT** for pillow top and pillow back
- 18-inch square pillow form
- **BLACK** and **GOLD** No.8 pearl cotton for decorative stitches
- freezer paper for appliqués
- template material (template plastic or cardstock)
- small, sharp scissors
- No. 7 embroidery needle
- 3/4-inch sequin pins (optional)
- fabric glue (optional)

Before beginning this project, read through General Instructions for Wool Appliqué on page 76 for complete instructions on how to prepare the wool and appliqué shapes.

Cutting

From STRIPE PRINT:

- Cut 1, 25 x 44-inch strip. From strip cut: 2, 18-1/2 x 25-inch rectangles for pillow back

- Cut 1, 18-1/2-inch square for pillow top (appliqué foundation)

From BLACK WOOL:

- Cut 3, F Circles

- Cut 2, G Circles

- Cut 1, H Circle

From GOLD WOOL:

- Cut 6, E Circles

- Cut 3, F Circles

- Cut 1, G Circle

From GREEN WOOL:

- Cut 4, F Circles

- Cut 3, G Circles

- Cut 1, H Circle

Wool Appliqué

Step 1   Mark a 2-inch border on all 4 sides of the 18-1/2-inch **STRIPE** pillow top square. The marked border will serve as a guide when placing circles.

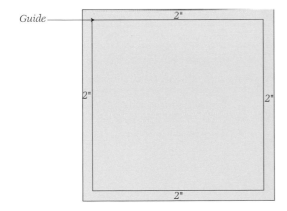

Step 2   Referring to the photograph on page 54 for placement, position the prepared wool circles on the pillow top. Blanket stitch circles in place with pearl cotton. Refer to *General Instructions for Wool Appliqué* on page 76 for complete instructions on appliquéing the circles in place.

Pillow Back

Step 1   With wrong sides together, fold each pillow back rectangle in half crosswise to make 2, 12-1/2 x 18-1/2-inch double-thick pillow back pieces. Overlap the 2 folded edges so pillow back measures 18-1/2-inches square. Pin pieces together and machine baste around entire piece using a 1/4-inch seam allowance to create a single pillow back.

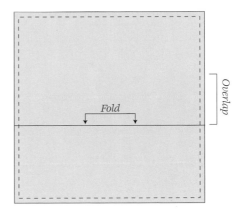

Step 2   With right sides together, layer the pillow back and the prepared pillow top; pin. Stitch around outside edges using a 1/2-inch seam allowance. Turn pillow cover right side out. Make sure corners are pushed out and square. Insert pillow form through back opening.

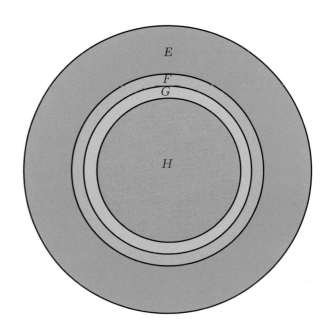

Double Bubble Band Pillow

Fabrics & Supplies

Finished Size: 16-inches square

Note: Extra yardage is allowed so the wool can be felted (prewashed). 100% wool can shrink up to 20% in width and length; a wool blend will shrink less. To avoid future shrinkage upon completion of your wool appliqué project, dry cleaning is recommended.

- (9) 5-inch squares of **ASSORTED WOOL** for circles

- 1-1/8 yards **MULTI-COLOR PRINT** for pillow top and pillow back

- 3/8 yard **STRIPE PRINT** for band (appliqué foundation)

- 16-inch square pillow form

- **BLACK** and **GOLD** No.8 pearl cotton for decorative stitches

- freezer paper for appliqués

- template material (template plastic or cardstock)

- small, sharp scissors

- No. 7 embroidery needle

- 3/4-inch sequin pins (optional)

- fabric glue (optional)

Before beginning this project, read through **General Instructions for Wool Appliqué** *on page 76 for complete instructions on how to prepare the wool and appliqué shapes.*

Cutting

From MULTI-COLOR PRINT:
- Cut 1, 22 x 44-inch strip. From strip cut:
  2, 16-1/2 x 22-inch rectangles for pillow back
- Cut 1, 16-1/2-inch square for pillow top

From STRIPE PRINT:
- Cut 1, 13 x 16-1/2-inch rectangle
  for appliqué foundation

From ASSORTED WOOL:
- Cut 17, C Circles
- Cut 17, D Circles

Wool Appliqué

Step 1   Center and appliqué the wool D circles to the wool C circles using the blanket stitch with **GOLD** pearl cotton. Refer to *General Instructions for Wool Appliqué* on page 76 for complete instructions on appliquéing the circles together.

Step 2   With right sides together, fold the 13 x 16-1/2-inch **STRIPE** rectangle in half lengthwise to make a 6-1/2 x 16-1/2-inch rectangle. Stitch a 1/4-inch seam along the long raw edges. Turn right side out, position the seam in the center of the band and press.

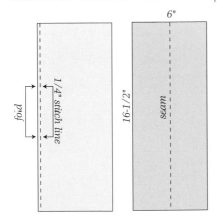

Step 3   Referring to the photograph on page 56 for placement, position the prepared wool circles on the 6 x 16-1/2-inch **STRIPE** band, starting 1-3/4-inches from the outside edges. Stagger the center row of circles between the top and bottom rows of circles. Appliqué

layered circles to band allowing 3/8-inch from top and bottom band edges. Blanket stitch in place with **BLACK** pearl cotton.

Step 4   Center the appliquéd band on the 16-1/2-inch square **MULTI-COLOR** pillow top. Machine-edge stitch the band in place.

Pillow Back

Step 1   With wrong sides together, fold each pillow back rectangle in half crosswise to make 2, 11 x 16-1/2-inch double-thick pillow back pieces. Referring to the diagram, overlap the 2 folded edges so pillow back measures 16-1/2 inches square. Pin pieces together and machine baste around entire piece using a 1/4-inch seam allowance to create a single pillow back.

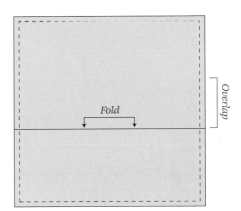

Step 2   With right sides together, layer the pillow back and the prepared pillow top; pin. Stitch around outside edges using a 1/2-inch seam allowance. Turn pillow cover right side out. Make sure corners are pushed out and square. Insert pillow form through back opening.

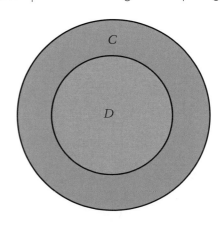

Garden Flower Woolie

Fabrics & Supplies

Finished Size: 12 x 18-inches

Note: Extra yardage is allowed so the wool can be felted (prewashed). 100% wool can shrink up to 20% in width and length; a wool blend will shrink less. To avoid future shrinkage upon completion of your wool appliqué project, dry cleaning is recommended.

- 1/2 yard **WHITE WOOL** for appliqué foundation and backing

- 1/4 yard **PURPLE WOOL** for circles and flower bases

- 1/4 yard **PINK WOOL** for flowers and circles

- 8-inch square *each* of 3 **COORDINATING GREEN WOOLS** for leaves and circles

- 6-inch square **YELLOW WOOL** for flower centers

- **PURPLE, GREEN** and **PINK** No.8 pearl cotton for decorative stitches

- freezer paper for appliqués

- template material (template plastic or cardstock)

- small, sharp scissors

- No. 7 embroidery needle

- 3/4-inch sequin pins (optional)

- fabric glue (optional)

- small amount of fiberfill for flower centers

Before beginning this project, read through General Instructions for Wool Appliqué on page 76 for complete instructions on how to prepare the wool and appliqué shapes.

Cutting

From WHITE WOOL:
- Cut 2 oval base shapes for top appliqué foundation and backing

From PURPLE WOOL:
- Cut 3, B Flower Bases on page 60
- Cut 23, C Circles on page 60

From PINK WOOL:
- Cut 3, 3/4 x 8-inch *bias* strips for flower center ruffles
- Cut 23, C Circles on page 60
- Cut 12, D Circles on page 60

From ASSORTED GREEN WOOL:
- Cut 6, A Leaves on page 60
- Cut 11, D Circles on page 60

From YELLOW WOOL:
- Cut 3, C Circles on page 60

Wool Appliqué

Step 1 Referring to photograph on page 62 for placement, position the **PURPLE** flower bases and **GREEN** leaves on the **WHITE** oval base for top appliqué foundation. Refer to *General Instructions for Wool Appliqué* on page 76 for complete instructions on appliquéing the shapes in place. Blanket stitch the shapes in place with matching pearl cotton.

Step 2 To make the **PINK** flower center ruffles, hand stitch a running basting stitch on (1) long edge of each 3/4 x 8-inch *bias* **PINK** strip. Pull up thread to gather strip as tightly as possible. Knot in place forming a tight circle of ruffled wool.

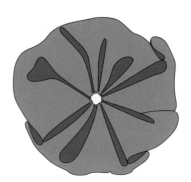

Step 3 To make the **YELLOW** flower centers, hand stitch a running basting stitch around the edge of each **YELLOW** C circle. Pull up thread to form a ball. Fill each ball with a small amount of fiberfill. Pull up thread tightly and knot in place.

Step 4 Hand stitch the **PINK** ruffles onto each **PURPLE** flower base. Hand stitch **YELLOW** flower center balls on top of each ruffle.

Step 5 Place the appliquéd **WHITE** oval on the **WHITE** backing oval. Blanket stitch the edges together with **PINK** pearl cotton.

Circle Border

Step 1 Blanket stitch **PINK** or **GREEN** D circles to **PURPLE** C circles with pearl cotton. Layer these circles on **PINK** C circles. Blanket stitch the edges together with **PURPLE** pearl cotton. Make 23 layered border circles.

Step 2 To attach the border circles, place the appliquéd **WHITE** oval unit face down on a flat surface. Mark the mid-point of each side of the **WHITE** oval to give you a guideline to accurately position the border circles. Place the border circles face down around the **WHITE** oval making sure they are evenly spaced.

Step 3 Place a pin connecting each border circle to the oval. Tack each border circle to the oval with 5 small whip stitches. Be sure to keep the oval flat while stitching and do not stitch through to the right side. Knot and bury the end of the thread by slipping your needle between the 2 layers of the oval. Cut the thread close to the fabric.

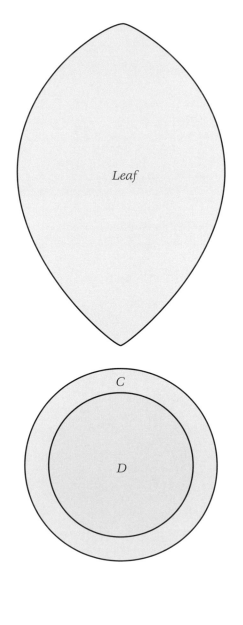

Leaf

C

D

Flower Base

Oval
Enlarge 140%

General Instructions
& Glossary

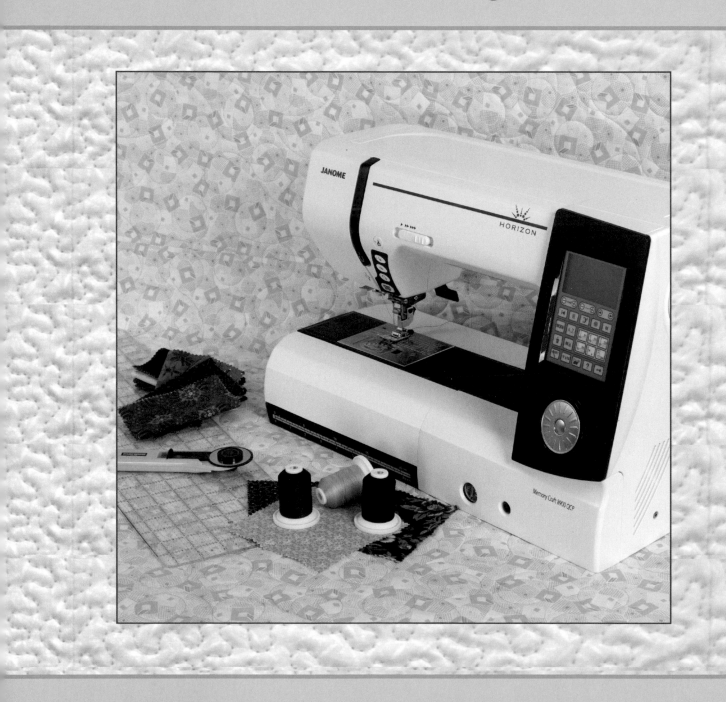

Getting Started

Yardage is based on 44-inch wide fabric. If your fabric is wider or narrower, it will affect the amount of necessary strips you need to cut in some patterns, and of course, it will affect the amount of fabric you have left over. Generally, Thimbleberries® patterns allow for a little extra fabric so you can confidently cut your pattern pieces with ease.

A rotary cutter, mat and wide clear acrylic ruler with 1/8-inch markings are needed tools in attaining accuracy. A beginner needs good tools just as an experienced quiltmaker needs good equipment. A 24 x 36-inch cutting mat is a good size to own. It will easily accommodate the average quilt fabrics and will aid in accurate cutting. The acrylic ruler you purchase should be at least 6 x 24-inches and easy to read. Do not purchase a smaller ruler to save money. The large size will be invaluable to your quiltmaking success.

It is often recommended to prewash and press fabrics to test for colorfastness and possible shrinkage. If you choose to prewash, wash in cool water and dry in a cool to moderate dryer. Industry standards actually suggest that line drying is best. Shrinkage is generally very minimal and usually is not a concern. A good way to test your fabric for both shrinkage and colorfastness is to cut a 3-inch square of fabric. Soak the fabric in a white bowl filled with water. Squeeze the water out of the fabric and press it dry on a piece of muslin. If the fabric is going to release color, it will do so either in the water or when it is pressed dry. Remeasure the 3-inch fabric square to see if it has changed size considerably (more than 1/4-inch). If it has, wash, dry and press the entire yardage. This little test could save you hours in prewashing and pressing.

Read instructions thoroughly before beginning a project. Each step will make more sense to you when you have a general overview of the whole process. Take one step at a time and follow the illustrations. They will often make more sense to you than the words. Take "baby steps" so you don't get overwhelmed by the entire process.

When working with flannel and other loosely woven fabrics, always prewash and dry. These fabrics almost always shrink more.

For piecing, place right sides of the fabric pieces together and use 1/4-inch seam allowances throughout the entire quilt unless otherwise specifically stated in the directions. An accurate seam allowance is the most important part of the quiltmaking process after accurately cutting. All the directions are based on accurate 1/4-inch seam allowances. It is very important to check your sewing machine to see what position your fabric should be in to get accurate seams. To test, use a piece of 1/4-inch graph paper, stitch along the quarter inch line as if the paper were fabric. Make note of where the edge of the paper lines up with your presser foot or where it lines up on the throat plate of your machine. Many quilters place a piece of masking tape on the throat plate to help guide the edge of the fabric. Next, test your seam allowance on fabric. Cut 2, 2-1/2-inch squares, place right sides together and stitch along one edge. Press seam allowances in one direction and measure. At this point the unit should measure 2-1/2 x 4-1/2-inches. If it does not, adjust your stitching guidelines and test again. Seam allowances are included in the cutting sizes given in this book.

Pressing is the third most important step in quiltmaking. As a general rule, you should never cross a stitched seam with another seam unless it has been pressed. Therefore, every time you stitch a seam, it needs to be pressed before adding another piece. Often, it will feel like you press as much as you sew, and often that is true. It is very important that you press and not iron the seams. Pressing is a firm, up-and-down motion that will flatten the seams but not distort the piecing. Ironing is a back-and-forth motion and will stretch and distort the small pieces. Most quilters use steam to help the pressing process. The moisture does help and will not distort the shapes as long as the pressing motion is used.

An old-fashioned rule is to press seam allowances in one direction, toward the darker fabric. Often, background fabrics are light in color and pressing toward the darker fabric prevents the seam allowances from showing through to the right side. Pressing seam allowances in one direction is thought to create a stronger seam. Also, for ease in hand quilting, the quilting lines should fall on the side of the seam which is opposite the seam allowance. As you piece quilts, you will find these "rules" to be helpful but not necessarily always appropriate. Sometimes seams need to be pressed in the opposite direction so the seams of different units will fit together more easily, which quilters refer to as seams "nesting" together. When sewing together two units with opposing seam allowances, use the tip of your seam ripper to gently guide the units under your presser foot. Sometimes it is necessary to re-press the seams to make the units fit together nicely. Always try to achieve the least bulk in one spot and accept that no matter which way you press, it may be a little tricky and it could be a little bulky.

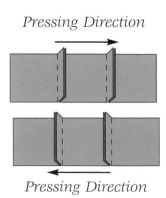

Pressing Direction

Pressing Direction

Squaring Up Blocks

To square up your blocks, first check the seam allowances. This is usually where the problem is, and it is always best to alter within the block rather than trim the outer edges. Next, make sure you have pressed accurately. Sometimes a block can become distorted by ironing instead of pressing.

To trim up block edges, use one of the many clear acrylic squares available on the market. Determine the center of the block; mark with a pin. Lay the square over the block and align as many perpendicular and horizontal lines as you can to the seams in your block. This will indicate where the block is off.

Do not trim all off on one side; this usually results in real distortion of the pieces in the block and the block design. Take a little fabric off all sides until the block is square. When assembling many blocks, it is necessary to make sure all are the same size.

Tools and Equipment

Making beautiful quilts does not require a large number of specialized tools or expensive equipment. My list of favorites is short and sweet and includes the things I use over and over again because they are always accurate and dependable.

I find a long acrylic ruler indispensable for accurate rotary cutting. The ones I like most are an Omnigrid® 6 x 24-inch grid acrylic ruler for cutting long strips and squaring up fabrics and quilt tops and a MasterPiece® 45-degree (8 x 24-inch) ruler for cutting 6- to 8-inch wide borders. I sometimes tape together two 6 x 24-inch acrylic rulers for cutting borders up to 12-inches wide.

A 15-inch Omnigrid® square acrylic ruler is great for squaring up individual blocks and corners of a quilt top, for cutting strips up to 15-inches wide or long and for trimming side and corner triangles.

I think the markings on my 24 x 36-inch Olfa® rotary cutting mat stay visible longer than on other mats, and the lines are fine and accurate.

The largest size Olfa® rotary cutter cuts through many layers of fabric easily, and isn't cumbersome to use. The 2-1/2-inch blade slices through three layers of backing, batting and a quilt top like butter.

An 8-inch pair of Gingher shears is great for cutting out appliqué templates and cutting fabric from a bolt or fabric scraps.

I keep a pair of 5-1/2-inch Gingher scissors by my sewing machine so it is handy for both machine work and handwork. This size is versatile and sharp enough to make large and small cuts equally well.

My Grabbit® magnetic pincushion has a surface that is large enough to hold lots of straight pins and a magnet strong enough to keep them securely in place.

Silk pins are long and thin, which means they won't leave large holes in your fabric. I like them because they increase accuracy in pinning pieces or blocks together. It is also easy to press over silk pins.

For pressing individual pieces, blocks and quilt tops, I use an 18 x 48-inch sheet of plywood covered with several layers of cotton fiberfill and topped with a layer of muslin stapled to the back. The 48-inch length allows me to press an entire width of fabric at one time without the need to reposition it, and the square ends are better than tapered ends on an ironing board for pressing finished quilt tops.

Using Grain

The fabric you purchase still has selvage and before beginning to handle or cut your fabric, it's helpful to be able to recognize and understand its basic characteristics. Fabric is produced in the mill with identifiable grain or direction. These are: lengthwise, crosswise and bias.

The lengthwise grain is the direction that fabric comes off the milling machine, and is parallel to the selvage. This grain of the fabric has the least stretch and the greatest strength.

The crosswise grain is the short distance that spans a bolt's 42-inch to 44-inch width. The crosswise grain, or width of grain, is between two sides called selvages. This grain of the fabric has medium stretch and medium strength.

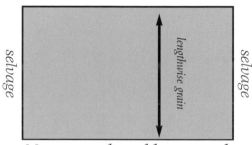

Most strength and least stretch

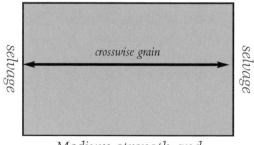

Medium strength and medium stretch

Avoiding Bias

The 45-degree angle on a piece of fabric is the bias and the direction with the most stretch. I suggest avoiding sewing on the bias until you're confident handling fabric. With practice and careful handling, bias edges can be sewn and are best for making curves.

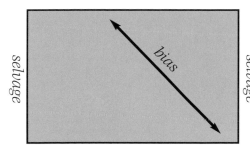

Least strength and most stretch

Rotary Cutting

SAFETY FIRST! The blades of a rotary cutter are very sharp, and need to be for accurate cutting. Look at a variety of cutters to find one that feels good in your hand. All quality cutters have a safety mechanism to "close" the cutting blade when not in use. After each cut and before laying the rotary cutter down, close the blade. Soon this will become second nature to you and will prevent dangerous accidents. Always keep cutters out of the sight of children. Rotary cutters are very tempting to fiddle with when they are laying around. When your blade is dull or nicked, change it. Damaged blades do not cut accurately and require extra effort that can also result in slipping and injury. Also, always cut away from yourself for safety.

Squaring Off Fabric

Fold the fabric in half lengthwise matching the selvage edges.

Square off the ends of your fabric before measuring and cutting pieces. This means that the cut edge of the fabric must be exactly perpendicular to the folded edge which creates a 90-degree angle. Align the folded and selvage edges of the fabric with the lines on the cutting board and place a ruled square on the fold. Place a 6 x 24-inch ruler against the side of the square to get a 90-degree angle. Hold the ruler in place, remove the square, and cut along the edge of the ruler. If you are left-handed, work from the other end of the fabric. Use the lines on your cutting board to help line up fabric, but not to measure and cut strips. Use a ruler for accurate cutting, always checking to make sure your fabric is lined up with horizontal and vertical lines on the ruler.

6 x 24" ruler

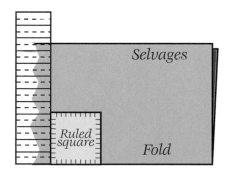

Cutting Strips

When cutting strips or rectangles, cut on the crosswise grain. Strips can then be cut into squares or smaller rectangles.

If your strips are not straight after cutting a few of them, refold the fabric, align the folded and selvage edges with the lines on the cutting board, and "square off" the edge again by trimming to straighten, and begin cutting.

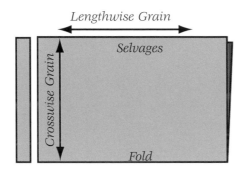

yes

no

Cutting Bias Strips

When cutting bias strips, trim your yardage on the crosswise grain so the edges are straight. With right sides facing up, fold the yardage on the diagonal. Fold the selvage edge (lengthwise grain) over to meet the cut edge (crosswise grain), forming a triangle.

This diagonal fold is the true bias. Position the ruler to the desired strip width from the cut edge and cut one strip. Continue moving the ruler across the fabric cutting parallel strips in the desired widths.

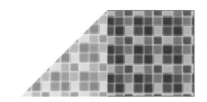

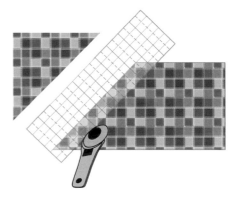

Trimming Side and Corner Triangles

In projects with side and corner triangles, the instructions have you cut side and corner triangles larger than needed. This will allow you to square up the quilt and eliminates the frustration of ending up with pre-cut side and corner triangles that don't match the size of your pieced blocks.

To cut triangles, first cut squares. The project directions will tell you what size to make the squares and whether to cut them in half to make two triangles or to cut them in quarters to make four triangles, as shown in the diagrams. This cutting method will give you side triangles that have the straight grain on the outside edges of the quilt. This is a very important part of quiltmaking that will help stabilize your quilt center.

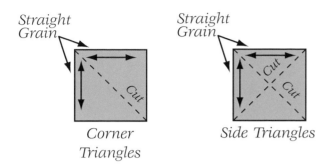

Straight Grain — *Corner Triangles*

Straight Grain — *Side Triangles*

Helpful Hints for Sewing with Flannel

Always prewash and machine dry flannel. This will prevent severe shrinkage after the quilt is made. Some flannels shrink more than others. For this reason, we have allowed approximately 1/4 yard extra for each fabric under the fabric requirements. Treat the more heavily napped side of solid flannels as the right side of the fabric.

Because flannel stretches more than other cotton calicos and because the nap makes them thicker, the quilt design should be simple. Let the fabric and color make the design statement.

Consider combining regular cotton calicos with flannels. The different textures complement each other nicely.

Use a 10 to 12 stitches per inch setting on your machine. A 1/4-inch seam allowance is also recommended for flannel piecing.

When sewing triangle-pieced squares together, take extra care not to stretch the diagonal seam. Trim off the points from the seam allowances to eliminate bulk.

Press gently to prevent stretching pieces out of shape.

Check block measurements as you progress. "Square up" the blocks as needed. Flannel will shift and it is easy to end up with blocks that are misshapen. If you trim and measure as you go, you are more likely to have accurate blocks. If you notice a piece of flannel is stretching more than the others, place it on the bottom when stitching on the machine. The natural action of the feed dogs will help prevent it from stretching.

Before stitching pieces, strips or borders together, pin often to prevent fabric from stretching and moving. When stitching longer pieces together, divide the pieces into quarters and pin. Divide into even smaller sections to get more control.

Use a lightweight batting to prevent the quilt from becoming too heavy.

Cutting Triangles from Squares

Cutting accurate triangles can be intimidating for beginners, but a clear acrylic ruler, rotary cutter and cutting mat are all that are needed to make perfect triangles. The cutting instructions often direct you to cut strips, then squares, and then triangles.

Sewing Layered Strips Together

When you are instructed to layer strips, right sides together, and sew, you need to take some precautions. Gently lay one strip on top of another, carefully lining up the raw edges. Pressing the strips together will hold them together nicely, and a few pins here and there will also help. Be careful not to stretch the strips as you sew them together.

Rod Casing or Sleeve to Hang Quilts

To hang wall quilts, attach a casing that is made of the same fabric as the quilt back. Attach this casing at the top of the quilt, just below the binding. Often, it is helpful to attach a second casing at the bottom of the quilt so you can insert a dowel into it which will help weight the quilt and make it hang free of ripples.

To make a rod casing or "sleeve," cut enough strips of fabric equal to the width of the quilt plus 2-inches for side hems. Generally, 6-inch wide strips will accommodate most rods. If you are using a rod with a larger diameter, increase the width of the strips.

Seam the strips together to get the length needed; press. Fold the strip in half lengthwise, wrong sides together. Stitch the long raw edges together with a 1/4-inch seam allowance. Center the seam on the backside of the sleeve; press. The raw edges of the seam will be concealed when the sleeve is stitched to the back of the quilt. Turn under both of the short raw edges; press and stitch to hem the ends. The final measurement should be about 1/2-inch from the quilt edges.

Pin the sleeve to the back of the quilt so the top edge of the sleeve is just below the binding. Hand stitch the top edge of the sleeve in place, then the bottom edge. Make sure to knot and secure your stitches at each end of the sleeve to make sure it will not pull away from the quilt with use. Slip the rod into the casing. If your wall quilt is not directional, making a sleeve for the bottom edge will allow you to turn your quilt end to end to relieve the stress at the top edge. You could also slip a dowel into the bottom sleeve to help anchor the lower edge of the wall quilt.

Hand stitch the sleeve to the quilt back

Hints and Helps for Pressing Strip Sets

When sewing strips of fabric together for strip sets, it is important to press the seam allowances nice and flat, usually to the darker fabric. Be careful not to stretch as you press, causing a "rainbow effect." This will affect the accuracy and shape of the pieces cut from the strip set. I like to press on the wrong side first and with the strips perpendicular to the ironing board. Then I flip the piece over and press on the right side to prevent little pleats from forming at the seams. Laying the strip set lengthwise on the ironing board seems to encourage the rainbow effect, as shown in the diagram.

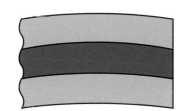

Avoid this rainbow effect

Borders

NOTE: Cut borders to the width called for in the directions. Always cut border strips a few inches longer than needed, just to be safe. Diagonally piece the border strips together as needed.

1. With pins, mark the center points along all 4 sides of the quilt. For the top and bottom borders, measure the 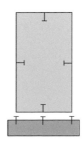 quilt from left to right through the middle.

2. Measure and mark the border lengths and center points on the strips cut for the borders before sewing them on.

3. Pin the border strips to the quilt and stitch a 1/4-inch seam. Press the seam allowances toward the border. Trim off excess border lengths.

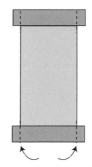

Trim away excess fabric

4. For the side borders, measure your quilt from top to bottom, including the borders just added, to determine the length of the side borders.

5. Measure and mark the side border lengths as you did for the top and bottom borders.

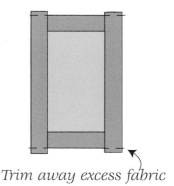

Trim away excess fabric

6. Pin and stitch the side border strips in place. Press and trim the border strips even with the borders just added.

7. If your quilt has multiple borders, measure, mark, and sew additional borders to the quilt in the same manner.

Decorative Stitches

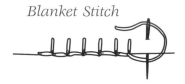

Blanket Stitch

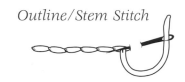

Outline/Stem Stitch

Straight Stitch

Crib — 45 x 60-inches

Approx. 40"
Approx. 40"

2-3/4 yards
Cut 2,
1-3/8 yard lengths

Twin — 72 x 90-inches

Approx. 40"   Approx. 40"
5-1/3 yards
Cut 2, 2-2/3 yard lengths

Double/Full — 81 x 96-inches

Approx. 40"
Approx. 40"
Approx. 40"

7-1/8 yards
Cut 3, 2-3/8 yard lengths

Queen—90 x 108-inches

Approx. 40"
Approx. 40"
Approx. 40"

8 yards
Cut 3, 2-2/3 yard lengths

Choosing the Backing

The backing of any quilt is just as important to the overall design as the pieced patchwork top. Combine large-scale prints or piece coordinating fabrics together to create an interesting quilt back. Using large pieces of fabric (perhaps three different prints that are the same length as the quilt) or a large piece of fabric that is bordered by compatible prints, keeps the number of seams to a minimum, which speeds up the process. The new 108-inch wide fabric sold on the bolt eliminates the need for seaming entirely. Carefully selected fabrics for a well-constructed backing not only complement a finished quilt, but make it more useful as a reversible accent.

Finishing the Quilt

1. Remove the selvages from the backing fabric. Sew the long edges together and press. Trim the backing and batting so they are 4-inches to 6-inches larger than the quilt top.

2. Mark the quilt top for quilting. Layer the backing, batting and quilt top. Baste the 3 layers together and quilt.

3. When quilting is complete, remove basting. Hand baste all 3 layers together a scant 1/4-inch from the edge. This hand basting keeps the layers

from shifting and prevents puckers from forming when adding the binding. Trim excess batting and backing fabric even with the edge of the quilt top. Add the binding as shown below.

Binding and Diagonal Piecing

1. Diagonally piece the binding strips. Fold the strip in half lengthwise, wrong sides together, and press.

Diagonal Piecing

Stitch diagonally   *Trim to 1/4-inch seam allowance*   *Press seam open*

Double-layer Binding

2. Unfold and trim one end at a 45-degree angle. Turn under the edge 3/8-inch and press. Refold the strip.

Fold line

3. With raw edges of the binding and quilt top even, stitch with a 3/8-inch seam allowance, starting 2-inches from the angled end.

4. Miter the binding at the corners. As you approach a corner of the quilt, stop sewing 3/8-inch from the corner of the quilt.

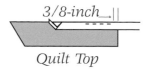

3/8-inch

Quilt Top

5. Clip the threads and remove the quilt from under the presser foot. Flip the binding strip up and away from the quilt, then fold the binding down even with the raw edge of the quilt. Begin sewing at the upper edge. Miter all 4 corners in this manner.

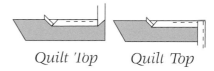

Quilt Top   *Quilt Top*

6. Trim the end of the binding so it can be tucked inside of the beginning binding about 1/2-inch. Finish stitching the seam.

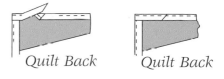

Quilt Back   *Quilt Back*

7. Turn the folded edge of the binding over the raw edges and to the back of the quilt so that the stitching line does not show. Hand sew the binding in place, folding in the mitered corners as you stitch.

Quilt Back   *Quilt Back*   *Quilt Back*

About Wool

The smallest amount of scrap wool can create wonderful decorative items. Combine wool with cotton fabrics from your stash as well as upholstery fabric scraps. The combination of the different textures makes the final project even more interesting. Stitching wool projects by hand isn't necessarily quick but it is so fun and can even be relaxing.

The variation within the stitches adds to the character of a true hand crafted item. A variety of threads can be used when hand stitching. Embroidery floss, pearl cotton (sizes 5, 8 and 12 are the most common) and even buttonhole twill can be used.

Experimenting with color and thread makes the projects unique and allows use of both fabric, wool and thread stashes. Wool appliqué adds a charming decorative touch to any decor.

General Instructions for Wool Appliqué

About our fabric requirements...extra yardage is allowed so the wool can be felted (prewashed). 100% wool can shrink up to 20% in width and length; a wool blend will shrink less. To avoid future shrinkage upon completion of your wool appliqué project, dry cleaning is recommended.

All Wool Should be Felted

- Felting wool (washing and drying) softens the fabric and interlocks the fibers. The felted wool is much less likely to ravel and it is perfect for making wool appliqué.

Tip: *Do not mix wool colors during the felting process.*

Felting by Hand (for smaller pieces)

- Boil the wool for 5 minutes using a few drops of detergent in the water. Squeeze out all excess moisture. Machine dry the wool with a bath towel at a moderately high temperature. Press if necessary.

Felting by Machine (for larger pieces)

- Run the wool through the gentle wash cycle with hot water and a small amount of detergent (1 teaspoon). Machine dry the wool with a bath towel at a moderately high temperature. Press if necessary.

Making Accurate Multiples of the Same Shape (Circles & Leaves)

Using a template is much faster and more accurate than tracing the shapes freehand.

- Trace the shape onto paper and cut out.

- Carefully trace the shape onto template material to make a template.

- Cut out the template on the line and trace the shape onto the dull side of the freezer paper.

Preparing Appliqué Shapes

With a pencil, trace the shapes onto the dull side of the freezer paper. Trace the shapes the number of times indicated and allow at least 1/4-inch between each shape. Cut the shapes apart, leaving a small margin beyond the drawn lines.

Press the shiny side of the freezer paper shapes onto the felted wool using a medium setting on your iron. Let the wool cool. Freezer paper releases easily so use a few pins to anchor the freezer paper securely to the wool on each appliqué shape.

Cut carefully and directly on the traced line using a small, sharp scissors. It is important to cut accurately. Remove and discard the freezer paper.

Tip: I recommend 3/4-inch sequin pins. They are less likely to catch your thread.

Blanket stitch layered elements together (i.e., small circles on larger circles) before attaching to the appliqué foundation. Use pins or a small amount of fabric glue to secure the appliqué shapes in place. As you stitch, the appliqué shapes tend to shift. Pinning or gluing the appliqué shapes together will keep them in place.

Attaching the Shapes to the Appliqué Foundation

Tip: It is always wise to plan ahead by arranging all the shapes on the appliqué foundation before stitching.

Adjust the shapes as necessary to match the photo. Remove all the pieces except those you are stitching. It is best to stitch the center pieces first. Pin or glue in place. Blanket stitch the shapes in place.

Stitching Appliqués

- Use pearl cotton, an embroidery needle and blanket stitch to appliqué the shapes.

Blanket Stitch

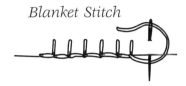

- Work with a long enough length of thread to eliminate the need to start a new thread while stitching an appliqué shape.

Glossary

Appliqué The sewing technique for attaching pieces (appliqués) of fabric onto a background fabric. Appliqués may be stitched to the background by hand, using a blind stitch, or by machine, using a satin stitch or a blind hemstitch.

Backing The bottom layer of a quilt consisting of one whole piece of fabric or several fabrics joined together.

Basting The technique for joining layers of fabric or the layers of a quilt with safety pins (pin basting) or large stitches (hand basting). The pinning or stitching is temporary and is removed after permanent stitching.

Batting A layer of filler placed between two pieces of fabric to form a quilt. Its thickness and fiber content varies.

Bias The grain of woven fabric that is at a 45-degree angle to the selvages. The bias grain has more stretch and is less stable than the crosswise or lengthwise grain.

Bias strips Strips of fabric cut on the bias and joined to make one continuous strip for binding that can easily be positioned around curved edges.

Binding The strip of fabric used to cover the outside edges—top, batting and backing—of a quilt.

Block A basic unit, usually square and often repeated, of a quilt top.

Borders The framing on a quilt that serves to visually hold in the design and give the eye a stopping point.

Crosscutting Cutting fabric strips into smaller units, such as squares or rectangles.

Crosswise grain The threads running perpendicular to the selvage across the width of a woven fabric.

Cutting mat Surface used for rotary cutting that protects the tabletop and keeps the fabric from shifting while cutting. Often mats are labeled as self-healing, meaning the blade does not leave slash marks or grooves in the surface even after repeated use.

Double-fold binding Binding made from a fabric strip that is folded in half before being attached to the quilt. Also, referred to as French-fold binding.

Finished size The measurement of a completed block or quilt.

Free-motion or machine quilting A process of quilting done with the feed dogs disengaged and using a darning presser foot so the quilt can be moved freely on the machine bed in any direction.

Grain The direction of woven fabric. The crosswise grain is from selvage to selvage. The lengthwise grain runs parallel to the selvage and is stronger. The bias grain is at a 45-degree angle and has the greatest amount of stretch.

Hand quilting Series of running stitches made through all layers of a quilt with needle and thread.

Hanging sleeve Tube of fabric that is attached to the quilt back. A wooden dowel is inserted through the fabric tube to hang the quilt. It is also called a rod pocket and used with a board or rod as a support to hang a quilt on the wall.

Inner border A strip of fabric, usually more narrow than the outer border, that frames the quilt center.

Layering Placing the quilt top, batting, and quilt backing on top of each other in layers.

Lengthwise grain The threads running parallel to the selvage in a woven fabric.

Longarm quilting A quilting machine used by professional quilters in which the quilt is held taut on a frame that allows the quilter to work on a large portion of the quilt at a time. The machine head moves freely, allowing the operator to use free-motion to quilt in all directions.

Machine quilting Series of stitches made through all layers of a quilt sandwich with a sewing machine.

Marking tools A variety of pens, pencils, and chalks that can be used to mark fabric pieces or a quilt top.

Mitered seam A 45-degree angle seam.

Outer border A strip of fabric that is joined to the edges of the quilt top to finish or frame it.

Pieced border Blocks or pieced units sewn together to make a single border unit that is then sewn to the quilt center.

Piecing The process of sewing pieces of fabric together.

Pressing Using an iron with an up and down motion to set stitches and flatten a seam allowance, rather than sliding it across the fabric.

Quilt center The quilt top before borders are added.

Quilt top Top layer of a quilt usually consisting of pieced blocks.

Quilting The small running stitches made through the layers of a quilt (quilt top, batting and backing) to form decorative patterns on the surface of the quilt and hold the layers together.

Quilting stencils Quilting patterns with open areas through which a design is transferred onto a quilt top. May be purchased or made from sturdy, reusable template plastic.

Rotary cutter Tool with a sharp, round blade attached to a handle that is used to cut fabric. The blade is available in different diameters.

Rotary cutting The process of cutting fabric into strips and pieces using a revolving blade rotary cutter, a thick, clear acrylic ruler, and a special cutting mat.

Running stitches A series of in-and-out stitches used in hand quilting.

Seam allowance The 1/4-inch margin of fabric between the stitched seam and the raw edge.

Selvage The lengthwise finished edge on each side of the fabric.

Slipstitch A hand stitch used for finishing, such as sewing binding to a quilt where the thread is hidden by slipping the needle between a fold of fabric and tacking down with small stitches.

Squaring up or straightening fabric The process of trimming the raw edge of the fabric so it creates a 90-degree angle with the folded edge of the fabric. Squaring up is also a term used when trimming a quilt block.

Strip sets Two or more strips of fabric, cut and sewn together along the length of the strips.

Triangle-pieced square The square unit created when two 90-degree triangles are sewn together on the diagonal.

Unfinished size The measurement of a block before the 1/4-inch seam allowance is sewn or the quilt is quilted and bound.